D1478866

Content Distribution Networks

Content Distribution Networks
An Engineering Approach

Dinesh C. Verma
IBM, T. J. Watson Research Center

A Wiley-Interscience Publication
JOHN WILEY & SONS, INC.

This text is printed on acid-free paper. ⊗

Copyright © 2002 by John Wiley & Sons, Inc., New York. All rights reserved.

Published simultaneously in Canada.

No part of this publication may be reproduced, stored in a retrieval system or transmitted in any form or by any means, electronic, mechanical, photocopying, recording, scanning or otherwise, except as permitted under Section 107 or 108 of the 1976 United States Copyright Act, without either the prior written permission of the Publisher, or authorization through payment of the appropriate per-copy fee to the Copyright Clearance Center, 222 Rosewood Drive, Danvers, MA 01923, (978) 750-8400, fax (978) 750-4744. Requests to the Publisher for permission should be addressed to the Permissions Department, John Wiley & Sons, Inc., 605 Third Avenue, New York, NY 10158-0012, (212) 850-6011, fax (212) 850-6008, E-Mail: PERMREQ @ WILEY.COM.

For ordering and customer service, call 1-800-CALL-WILEY

Library of Congress Cataloging-in-Publication Data is available.

ISBN 0-471-44341-7

Printed in the United States of America

10 9 8 7 6 5 4 3 2 1

621.3981
V 532c

*My wonderful wife Paridhi
and adorable children, Archit and Riya*

Contents

Preface

The field of computer networking has seen a dramatic change in its nature over the last few decades. In the early 1970s, computer networks tended to be a relatively specialized field with only a few experts at select universities and within the computer industry. There were a few scattered computer networks, mainly owned by large corporations, and some experimental university networks. In the last decade of the twentieth century, computer networks have become much more ubiquitous, and the Internet has become a household word. There are many more networks today, and the older existing networks (e.g., the public Internet) are much larger and more complex.

Although this increase in the size, number, and complexity of computer networks has enabled the deployment of many new applications, it has a downside as well. As networks become larger, more complex, and support more traffic, the performance of networked applications becomes more unpredictable and often unacceptable. Thus, a conscious effort needs to be made to improve the performance of networked applications, a term which can be loosely interpreted to include all applications consisting of two or more components communicating over a computer network. Thus, techniques that can improve the performance of a networked application need to be explored in more detail.

This book is about such a technique: content distribution networks, also known as content delivery networks, intelligent Internet infrastructure, and enhanced surrogate services. A content distribution network employs many geographically distributed sites to improve the scalability and client response time of applications. Content distribution networks offer certain advantages over alternative approaches to managing performance of networked applications, and hold a lot of promise for improving their performance.

This book explains the functioning of a content distribution network. It describes the components that make up a content distribution network, the different technologies that can be used within a content distribution network, and a description of some web-based applications that can be accelerated by using a content distribution network.

WHO WILL BENEFIT FROM THIS BOOK?

This book is intended for researchers, students, and network practitioners who are interested in content distribution networks. If you are a graduate student or network researcher who wants to learn the different technologies that are used in content distribution networks, you will find this book very useful. This book contains a detailed description of all technologies relevant to a content distribution network.

If you are a network operator who operates a corporate intranet, you will find the description contained in this book very helpful. It will teach you how access to many of the intranet applications can be improved using content distribution technologies.

If you are work for an ISP, and are interested in developing a content distribution solution for your customers, you will find this book of use. You will learn the different technologies that can be used for content distribution networks, and get an overview of their relative merits and demerits.

If you operate a website, this book will help you determine if the use of content distribution technologies can help you in improving your application's performance. It will also provide you with an "under the hood" look at how the content distribution offerings work.

If you work for one of the many companies that provide content distribution solutions, you will find this book of use in understanding the other possible choices that can be used to develop a content distribution network. This will provide you with a better understanding of your position with respect to the other alternatives.

Finally, if you are thinking about launching a new start-up related to content distribution networks, you will find this book to be a good review of related technologies. It will illustrate all the building blocks that make up a content distribution network and will help you in developing your own software and solutions.

WHO IS THIS BOOK NOT FOR?

This book is not intended to provide information about the content distribution solution provided by any specific vendor or company. If you want to find out how a specific company operates its content distribution networks, this book is not for you. Nor does this book offer a relative comparison of the solutions offered by specific vendors. However, the information given in this book can help you understand the merits and demerits of a specific vendor's solution.

This book is focused on content distribution networks that are used for improving the performance of networked applications, e.g., improving the response time of a website. There is another set of content distribution networks that enable sharing of content among multiple users (e.g., software used by Napster or Gnutella). These types of content distribution networks are not the primary focus of this book, and they are only discussed briefly in the last chapter. If you are looking for a detailed discussion of such networks, this book is not for you.

Finally, this book does not address any standards related to content distribution networks. At the time of writing this book, such standards were in a state of flux. If you are looking for an overview of the standards and protocols related to content distribution networks, or need information about the activities of any industry consortium or standards body related to content distribution, this book is not for you. However, this book will help you understand some of the technologies that underlie those standards.

ORGANIZATION OF THE BOOK

The material in this book is organized into eight chapters. Chapter 1 provides an overview of content distribution networks and compares it to other approaches for managing the performance of web-based applications. It also discusses how a content distribution solution is applicable in different business environments, e.g., when deployed within an enterprise intranet, offered by a network operator to its customers, or offered as a service on the public Internet. It also proposes a basic architecture for content distribution networks. This architecture is developed further in the subsequent chapters.

Chapter 2 provides an overview of a typical server site that is used to host web-based applications. It discusses the different schemes that can be used to improve the scalability of a server site.

Chapter 3 provides an overview of the different technologies that can be used to direct clients to different sites within a content distribution network. This includes a description of commonly deployed domain-name-based techniques as well as other techniques that can potentially be used to build viable alternatives.

Chapter 4 provides an overview of the performance monitoring that needs to be done in order to exploit content distribution networks to their fullest potential. Such performance monitoring data is a prerequisite for the client direction schemes described in Chapter 3.

Chapter 5 provides an overview of different technologies that can be used to manage the integrity and consistency of data that is distributed at the various surrogate servers that build up a content distribution network. It also discusses the different ways in which these schemes can improve network effectiveness.

Chapter 6 discusses the different types of interconnection arrangements that can be created between the different sites that make up a content distribution network. It also considers several issues that arise in managing security and trust relationships within a content distribution network. It includes a discussion of the topics of configuring and tracking usage of the content distribution network infrastructure.

Chapter 7 discusses some sample applications whose performance can be improved by deploying them on a content distribution network. It also discusses the nature of applications that can benefit from content distribution networks, and the nature of applications that are not likely to benefit much from content distribution networks.

Chapter 8 discusses some of the advanced topics related to content distribution networks. It includes a discussion of standards related to content distribution and a discussion of application layer, ad hoc content distribution networks (like Napster or Gnutella).

The writing of this book was made possible by a tremendous amount of support from many people, and I would like to express my deep appreciated to all those who have helped me in this process, especially to my family who supported me so strongly. I am also indebted to my wonderful colleagues at IBM Research, who have taught me much of what I know about content distribution networks. Colleagues whom I would like to thank specially are Anees Shaikh, Arvind Krishna, Dakshi Agrawal, Dilip Kandlur, David Lindquist, James Giles, Khalil Amiri, Marcia Peters, Madhu Chetuparambil, Rajesh Agarwalla, Renu Tewari, and Seraphin Calo.

1 Overview of Content Distribution Networks

1.1 INTRODUCTION

At the turn of the twenty-first century, computer networks and particularly networks based on the Internet Protocol (IP) have gained wide social acceptance. In addition to the public Internet, web-based applications over an IP intranet have become the norm for corporate internal networks and many business-to-business interactions. Few technologies have seen comparable acceptance and explosive growth. Unfortunately, this growth has also resulted in serious performance problems and degraded user experience for a large set of applications. The pejorative term often used for the World Wide Web, namely the World Wide Wait, is not without justification. Techniques that ensure satisfactory performance of networked applications become important in such an environment.

One approach to improving the performance of networked applications involves using many sites located at different points within the network. Some of these sites may be stand-alone servers or a single router with comparable functions. When a client attempts to access the main server site for an application, it is directed to one of the other sites. Each site caches information so that it has a high probability of servicing client requests without having to go back to the main server site. By accessing a closely located site, users can bypass the potential congestion that may lie on the path to the main server. The set of sites that are used to improve the performance of web-based applications collectively forms the content distribution network (CDN), which is the focus of this book.

In this first chapter of the book, I provide a very high level view of content distribution networks and the components that make up a content distribution network. Since the goal of content distribution networks is to improve the performance of networked applications, I start by examining the reasons why some applications might be slow. I also provide a brief overview of some other techniques (besides CDNs) that have been used or proposed for alleviating the performance problems of web-based applications. Then I look at the CDN solution and how it may be used to advantage in different types of network environments. Finally, I provide a description of the various components that make up a CDN. Each of these components will be further discussed in subsequent chapters.

1.2 PERFORMANCE ISSUES IN
NETWORKED APPLICATIONS

Figure 1.1 shows a simple model of the environment in which a user accesses a networked application. The user has a client software (e.g., a web browser) at his PC or desktop. He connects to the backbone network using the client access network. The backbone network connects him to a server network, where a server machine is running the application the user is trying to access. In or-

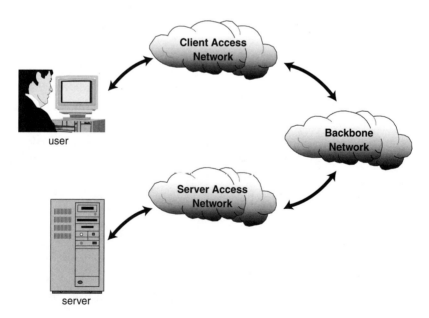

Figure 1.1.

der to access his application, the user needs to go through three network segments, the client access network, the backbone network, and the server access network. He also uses the processing capacity of two machines, one running the client software, and the other running the server application. In practice, the server network may use more than one machine to service the request. However, in order to understand the performance issues, let us consider the simple case when there is only one server.

Many real-life situations can be mapped onto the simple model presented above. Let us consider a web surfer accessing the Internet from his home. The web surfer dials into his local ISP (Internet service provider to obtain access to the Internet. His goal is to access a specific website, e.g., www.wiley.com. In this case, the client access network consists of the dial-in access to the web surfer's ISP network. The backbone network consists of the public network, and the server access network consists of the systems used by John Wiley & Sons, Inc. to host its website. Consider another situation in which a corporation has deployed a web-based application on its corporate intranet. The corporation consists of several locations, each location with its own local area network. The application server is deployed at one of these locations. Let us assume that the application is deployed at a location on the West Coast of the United States, and another user from a location on the East Coast is trying to access the application. The client access network would be the local area network at the East Coast site, the server access network would be the local area network at the West Coast site, and the intervening intranet connecting the different locations makes up the backbone network.

Let us assume that the user interacts with the server by issuing requests, and the server returns a response for each request. The response time of the application as seen by the user is the time interval that elapses between the issuance of the request and the receipt of the response. For example, the response time of a web access is the time it takes for a client to view a web page after typing in the URL at the browser. The user response time is a reasonably good metric to measure the performance of the networked application. For any given application, there is a best-case performance, which is normally obtained when the user is accessing the application over a network with no other traffic. Thus, the user gets the best performance possible for this application. This response time seen by the user in the best-case performance scenario depends on the design of the application and the characteristics of the network.

If an application's best-case performance is not satisfactory, then the application has not been designed properly for its operating environment. One can either change the application, or change the operating environment to bring the best-case performance within acceptable bounds. As an example, consider the case of a web page that is to be accessed by users over a dial-up modem link of 28.8 kbps in a normal environment. Let us assume that the modem has an effective throughput of 24 kbps and that the web page along with its associated graphics is approximately 240 Kbytes. This page would take about 80 seconds to download. This may not be acceptable. One can either change the application by redesigning the web page to use fewer graphics, or change the operating environment, e.g., have users access the application via faster access lines. If the page has been redesigned so that it (along with associated graphics) uses only 24 Kbytes, it can be downloaded in approximately 8 seconds. The other option would be to ensure that users access it via a leased T1 line, in which case the original page could be downloaded in a couple of seconds. If the application is designed for use on a corporate intranet, the latter option may be the preferred and feasible approach. On the other hand, if the web page is meant for home users via the public Internet, then the first option is the only viable one. Most application developers try their best to ensure that their users will have a reasonable response time under normal operating conditions.

The best-case scenario provides a lower bound on the response time that a user may experience. In practice, the actual response time seen by a user is likely to be worse than the best-case scenario. This is because other applications or users may be concurrently active on the network. This reduces the effective bandwidth available to an individual user on the network, and also reduces the share of processing cycles received at the machines. We will assume that applications are designed so that the best-case performance would be quite acceptable to the typical user. Therefore, the primary objective of managing performance on the network is to ensure that the degradation in application performance due to interfering traffic is within acceptable bounds.

If an application is experiencing serious degradation in performance from the best-case scenario, it is very likely that this is caused by interfering cross-traffic.* The problem may be that one of the network links is getting more traffic than it can handle quickly, or perhaps one of the machines (routers or servers) involved in the networked application is overwhelmed by requests it is receiving. These elements are the performance bottlenecks within the network. The basic approach to improving the performance of the applications is to eliminate or avoid the bottlenecks.

There are several methods for avoiding or eliminating performance bottlenecks within the network. These methods include capacity planning, Quality of Service mechanisms, and, of course, content distribution networks. Capacity planning consists of predicting the expected load on the different network elements and ensuring that none of the elements are overloaded. In other words, all network links are provisioned with enough capacity so that no link ever becomes congested and applications are executed at servers that are fast enough so as to never become overloaded. Another approach consists of deploying Quality of Service (QoS) mechanisms within the network. The QoS approach concedes that there will always be some cases in which the network links and server will be overwhelmed by the demand from network applications. Under these conditions, this approach ensures that some set of preferred applications do not see a degradation in their performance. This is achieved by using techniques like reservation or priorities within the network, even though other applications are not performing well.

1.2.1 Capacity Planning

The basic approach used in capacity planning is that of eliminating bottlenecks. If the performance of an application is not acceptable, there must be one or more performance bottlenecks within the system. If the bottleneck is a network link, one can increase its capacity until it no longer remains a bottleneck. Similarly, if the bottleneck is a machine, it can be upgraded to a faster one, or perhaps augmented by another machine that can share some of the processing load.

---

*Other reasons for poor performance might be a misconfigured network, a poorly managed network, or some type of software glitch affecting the network protocols. However, in most networks managed by competent administrators, these occurrences should have a relatively low probability.

In order to do a good job at capacity planning, one first needs to make an estimate of the total amount of traffic expected within the system. If a reasonably accurate estimate of the traffic at each network link can be obtained, one can then plan to have a new link in place with adequate capacity to satisfy the traffic demand. Similarly, if a reasonable estimate of the processing cycles needed by an application is obtained, then one can have appropriate servers or clusters of servers that can satisfy the requisite demand.

As an example, consider a network that is established for a hypothetical supermarket. For simplicity's sake, assume that the supermarket has only one outlet store and an office located in the same city. The office location hosts the computers that are used to process the various transactions at the outlet. The outlet is connected to the office via a link with a capacity of 45 Mbps. This situation is shown in Figure 1.2 (note the similarity to Figure 1.1; here the backbone network has been replaced by a link). The supermarket collects monthly statistics about the bandwidth utilized on this link. These statistics show that the amount of bandwidth needed is growing at the rate of 10% every month. The present average bandwidth used during the busiest hour on the link is 36 Mbps. Table 1.1 shows the expected bandwidth utilization for the next 4 months. At the expected growth rate, the link

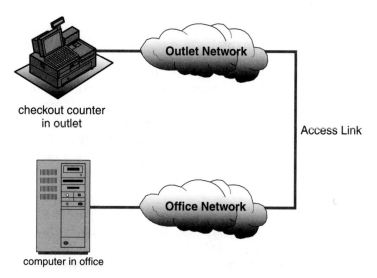

Figure 1.2.

Table 1.1   Expected bandwidth usage on supermarket link

Month	Expected bandwidth usage
0	36 Mbps
1	39.6 Mbps
2	43.6 Mbps
3	47.9 Mbps
4	52.1 Mbps

capacity will not be adequate after 3 months. Therefore, the supermarket decided to upgrade the link to the next higher available capacity, namely 155 Mbps. This upgrade would be sufficient to meet the expected bandwidth demand for the next 14 months. Capacity planning can also be used for determining if the processing capacity in routers and servers in the network needs to be increased.

As long as the growth in bandwidth requirements or the processing cycles required for any installation can be predicted reasonably accurately, capacity planning can be applied successfully. For environments in which the demands for traffic and processing power changes at a predictable rate, one can plan ahead to have adequate capacity within the network. As long as there is sufficient link capacity and processing power within the network, most applications can be expected to have a performance reasonably close to their best-case scenario.

The effectiveness of capacity planning depends significantly on the accuracy of the traffic prediction. If the traffic has an unanticipated surge, then the capacity provided within the network may not be adequate to ensure good performance. Many websites have encountered such an unexpected growth when they have engaged in promotional activity that has suddenly drawn a large number of people. A website may encounter this rapid growth in traffic (sometimes known as a flash-crowd) due to many factors—an advertisement that runs during a very popular televised event, e.g., the superbowl in the United States, a news-event that is related to the products offered by the website, or a favorable reference by a prominent media personality. Capacity planning is based on an estimate of how much traffic is expected at a site, and if the estimate proves to be incorrect, the performance experienced by the site is likely to degrade. Sometimes the traffic load is predictable, but simply growing too fast. For example, one might be able to estimate that the traffic growth is increasing so rapidly that an upgrade in the link capacity is needed within 3 days. However, if the link provider takes a week to install the new line, the new link cannot be upgraded quickly enough to avoid the anticipated overload.

Another factor that limits the effectiveness of capacity planning is the variability of traffic load. Capacity planning is often done on the basis of the average load on a link or a server. However, the load may show variations that are dependent on factors such as the time of day or the day of the week. A supermarket network is likely to be busier on weekends than on weekdays. Also, on a weekday, there would be more traffic in the evening hours than during other times of the day. In order to have adequate capacity within the network, one often uses the busiest hour in order to plan the capacity of the network. Even then, there are issues associated with the variability of the average load during the busiest hour. Consider Figure 1.3, which shows the traffic load averaged during the busiest hour for two different supermarkets over a one-month period. Both of these supermarkets have the same average traffic load of approximately 36 Mbps during the

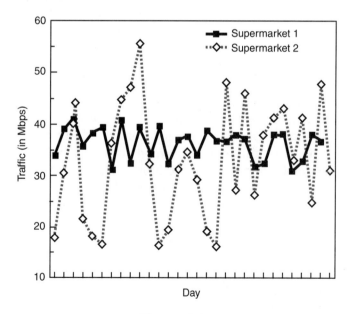

Figure 1.3.

busy period. However, there is significantly more variability in the traffic load experienced by the second supermarket than the first. If we use the same type of network link for supporting both the supermarkets, the second one is likely to see more instances of bad performance.

One way to work around the problem is to select capacity of the links that is not based on the average value, but on another metric that takes the variability into account. As an example, one can choose to select the 90th percentile of the observed values. The 90th percentile is a value selected such that 90% of the observed data points are below it. This approach will dictate that the second supermarket in Figure 1.3 use higher-capacity links than the first super-market. Variability should be taken into account when doing capacity planning. However, if the variability is too high, this approach can result in a fairly expensive solution.

Capacity planning is fundamentally a technique for estimating the normal operating environment and planning for resources accordingly. It is not very efficient at taking care of things that are not normally expected. In an environment where a traffic surge is expected with a relatively small probability, capacity planning's approach would be to ignore the unlikely circumstances and plan around the normal operating averages (with some accommodation for variability). However, if these low-probability surges are significant events, then one must select an approach that can provide a cost-effective solution to them.

Several texts explain the principles of capacity planning [1–4]. Information on designing a network in response to specific traffic loads can be found in books written from a theoretical perspective [5], an algorithmic perspective [6, 7] or an applied, practical perspective [8, 9].

1.2.2 Quality of Service

The basic assumption behind the Quality of Service approach is that one can never have enough resources within the network. No matter how good a job one does at estimating and installing the required capacity within the network, all the excess capacity gets used up for one reason or another. The surplus capacity may be used up by new applications coming on line, new users coming on line, or simply by growth in the bandwidth used by the current set of users and applications.

If surplus capacity cannot be assumed, then it is not possible to offer acceptable performance to all of the traffic flows that are active within the network. A traffic flow is loosely defined as a user trying to access an application over the network. However, it may be possible to protect the performance of some set of traffic flows at the expense of other flows. The QoS approach is an attempt to protect the performance of some subset of traffic flows in the network. Two approaches to QoS are commonly used; the first relies on reserving resources within the network in order to ensure adequate capacity to meet the performance requirements of a traffic flow, and the second simply places flows into one or more classes, with some getting preferential treatment over the others.

1.2.2.1 The Reservation Approach.

The reservation approach to assuring performance is implemented in the ATM [10] protocols and in the Integrated Services [11] specifications related to the IP protocol. The basics of the reservation approach is that applications inform the network about the amount of resources they need for adequate performance within the network. The resource requirement information is exchanged using a signaling protocol. The signaling is normally done before actual data transfer begins, but an application can also start data transfer and the signaling process concurrently, with an expectation that the signaling process would be successful.

The signaling process sends messages over the nodes that would be involved in the communication and states the amount of resources that would be needed by a flow. Each node would reserve the requisite amount of resources, or decline the resource reservation request. If all of the nodes along the path allow the reservation, then the requisite resources are allocated to the traffic flow for its duration. This ensures that the flow would have good performance if the signaling process succeeded.

Although the reservation approach can be used to provide performance guarantees, there have been several problems hindering its adoption. One major problem is that most signaling protocols turn out to be quite complex and inefficient, especially when all the possible error cases (lost messages, route changes, etc.) are taken into account. Furthermore, the traffic flow to which a data packet belongs needs to be determined at each switch. In a connection-oriented architecture, this is not too difficult. In connectionless architectures like IP, identifying the flows to which each data packet belongs imposes serious performance penalties.

1.2.2.2 The Class Differentiation Approach

The second approach to QoS does not require an explicit signaling protocol, and thus is significantly simpler than the reservation-based approach. This scheme classifies all the packets entering into the network into two or more classes of service. The class information of each packet is encoded into the packet in some fashion. Each of the classes is associated with specific resources. Each switch in the network can easily determine the class of the packet, and decide how much resources to allocate to that packet.

The most simple instance of differentiated classes are networks that offer two or more priority levels. One class of traffic always takes precedence over the other class. When there is congestion at one of the links, the performance of the higher-precedence class is less likely to be degraded, whereas the performance of the lower-precedence class is more likely to be degraded. Such priority schemes are found in many network architectures, e.g., in the network priority fields of IBM SNA [12] networks.

A more complex and sophisticated version of this approach is used in the IP differentiated services architecture [13]. In this approach, a set of edge routers marks a field in the IP header indicating the class of the packet. Each class of packet marking corresponds to specific types of processing at intermediate routers, the specific type of processing being referred to as a PHB (per-hop behavior). A PHB can be assigned with complex resource reservation, including limits on bandwidth used by a class, priority in access to switch buffers, or priority in being scheduled for transmission. The net effect, again, is to use some of the network resources preferentially for one set of traffic flows as compared to others.

The differentiation approach offers a solution that is much simpler than the reservations approach. However, it does not provide any assurances about the performance of any class. Even the highest-priority class may have poor performance if there are a lot of high-priority traffic flows within the network.

QoS architectures have been around for quite a while, but are rarely deployed in networks. In the context of IP networks, actual QoS deployments are almost unheard of. The main challenge facing the QoS approach is that it requires an upgrade of the entire networking infrastructure; all switches need to support reservations or service differentiation in order for it to be effective. This upgrade poses a significant logistic challenge in any operational network. Another complicating factor is deciding which set of traffic flows ought to get preferred performance and which ones should not. The determination and enforcement of these policies is a daunting task in any real deployment of QoS. Furthermore, in an environment like the Internet, where any communication crosses multiple administrative domain boundaries, QoS must be enabled across all of the administrative domains in order to be effective. The chances of such ubiquitous support of QoS becoming available in the Internet in the near term are fairly remote.

More information on reservation-based approaches within the Internet can be found in the text by Ferguson and Huston [14], and a description of service differentiation can be found in the text by Kilkki [15].

1.3   CONTENT DISTRIBUTION NETWORKS OVERVIEW

Content distribution networks provide the third approach to solving the performance issues in a congested network. Their basic goal is to avoid the congested links within the network. If a client-to-server communication does not traverse a portion of the network that is congested, it is likely to have good performance. If the path does happen to be congested, it might be possible for a client to get its services from a secondary server (which we will refer to as a surrogate server) with better performance.

The basic concept behind a content distribution network is illustrated in Figure 1.4. It shows the familiar picture of a client trying to access a server across a backbone network. The path that is used between the client and the server is congested, as shown by the curved line connecting the client and the server in the figure. Suppose, however, that there is another server (called the surrogate server) within the network, with which the client has better connectivity, and the client can obtain all the information it needs by contacting the surrogate server instead of the original server. In this case, the client might obtain better performance if it connects to the site containing the surrogate server instead of the original server.

If we can direct a client to communicate with the surrogate

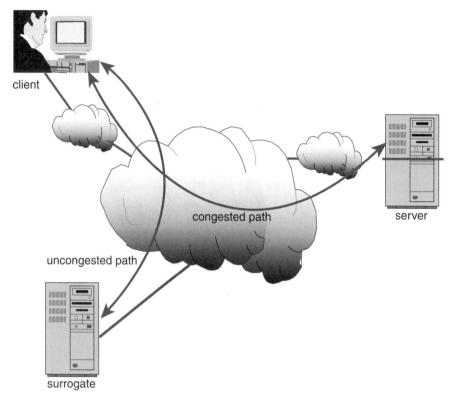

Figure 1.4.

server, and set up a system in which the surrogate server can handle a large portion of the client's request, we will avoid the congested part of the communication link and improve the user-perceived response time. Of course, any surrogate server will have good connectivity only with a few client users. If we want to extend this solution to most of the clients, we will need to have more than one surrogate within the network. This situation is depicted in Figure 1.5. It shows three group of clients, each of which is directed to a separate surrogate server. The original server may be used to handle any remaining clients in the system.

Figure 1.5 illustrates a typical content distribution network. The content distribution network (shown as a dotted cloud in the figure) consists of many surrogate sites located so that it is highly likely that a client has good connectivity to at least one of the sur-

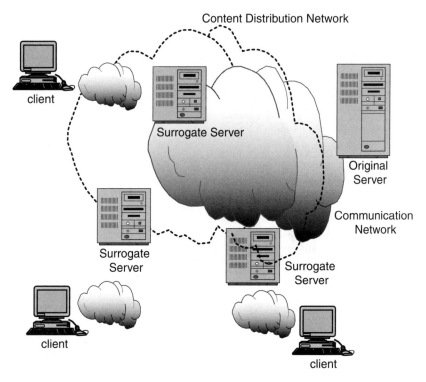

Figure 1.5.

rogate sites. Each client is directed to one of such sites, and obtains good performance even if the path between the client and the original server is congested. Each surrogate site may contain a single surrogate server or many surrogate servers that cooperate with each other. This approach avoids the congestion that can arise in the network, and can result in better performance for the client. Another benefit of the content distribution network is that the processing capacity of the surrogate servers is added to that of the original server, which results in the ability to handle many more clients than the original server might be capable of handling by itself. Thus, a content distribution network can significantly improve the scalability of any networked application. Another advantage of content distribution networks is an improvement in application reliability. Even when the main server is down, one of the surrogates may be able to provide data to the client, thereby improving the availability of the application.

1.3.1 Effectiveness of Content Distribution Networks

The content distribution network described above can avoid congested portions of the network completely if it is able to get all of its services from the surrogate sites. The effectiveness of the approach is therefore heavily dependent on the probability that the surrogate is actually able to satisfy the client's request. If the client's request cannot be satisfied by the surrogate server, the surrogate may need to go back to the original server in order to fulfill the request made by the client. It is highly likely that the path from the surrogate to the original server shares some links with the path that the client uses to communicate with the original server, and is probably congested. Thus, every time the surrogate is not able to satisfy the requests from the client, the performance will be poor. The performance perceived by the client when going to the original server via the surrogate is likely to be worse than if it went directly to the original server. After all, the surrogate site adds some latency to the request handling, and serves no function other than acting as a relay.

Thus, the effectiveness of the content distribution network is highly dependent on the hit ratio that can be supported by the surrogate. The hit ratio is the probability that a client's request will be completely satisfied by the surrogate. In applications where this hit ratio is very high, the content distribution networks are likely to result in an improved response time for the end-user. In applications where the hit ratio is poor, the content distribution networks are not likely to be of use.

Traffic flows in most applications deal with transfer of data between a client and a server. Such exchanged data may be static or dynamic. Static data is defined as data that does not change, or changes very slowly. Dynamic data is data that is likely to change at relatively faster. The definition of fast/slow depends on the characteristics of the link between the surrogates and the main server.

Applications typically exchange a mix of static and dynamic data during their execution. If the mix contains predominantly static data, then its performance can be readily improved using a content distribution network. In these cases, the surrogate caches the static data and provides it to the client as needed. However, if the mix consists predominantly of dynamic data, the surrogates need to ensure that the copy of the data that they have is consistent with the current version present at the original server. Managing the consistency of data is an overhead that can adversely affect the benefits of a content distribution network. Not all dynamic data can be efficiently maintained at surrogate sites. However, some types of dynamic data can indeed be efficiently maintained at the surrogate server, and the performance of a large number of applications can be improved using content distribution networks.

One drawback of a content distribution network is its manageability. A CDN consists of many sites that are geographically distributed. These sites need to be managed and administered, and such administration is much more complex and costly than managing a set of servers at a single location. Therefore, content distribution networks should be designed with a strong emphasis on the manageability of the surrogate servers and surrogate sites.

Another drawback of content distribution networks is that applications may need to be redesigned in order to exploit the existence of surrogates. Such a redesign may not be an issue in the case of many applications, but can pose a real challenge for others. Applications that are being newly developed can indeed be written to exploit a CDN. However, existing applications may need some changes before they can use the surrogate servers. One way to introduce these changes is to put a reverse surrogate server in front of the application server. The reverse surrogate server introduces the required modifications. Another way would be to modify the application. If an existing application is being modified, such changes require additional time for testing and removing bugs. The implications of such changes should be analyzed before deploying a content-distribution-network-based solution.

1.3.2   Applications Suitable for a CDN

Many types of applications have characteristics that make them a good match for content distribution networks. Most commercial offerings of content distribution networks are based on the web. Web browsing has a large component of static data, e.g., images, static HTML files, etc., and is a good candidate for a CDN. Some types of dynamic data encountered in web browsing, e.g., data created based on the identity or profile of a user or results of some common queries obtained via the web, can also be improved easily using a CDN approach. Retrieval of large static files, e.g., music clips or video images, can be improved significantly by deploying them on a CDN. In addition to these applications, one can use CDNs to improve the performance of many web-based shopping stores, as well as reduce the time it takes to show banner advertisements on a web page.

Web-based applications are not the only ones that can benefit from CDN. Traditional Internet-based services, e.g., file transfer (ftp) servers or mail servers, can also benefit from the use of replication and surrogate servers. Access to directory services can be improved by using a CDN, and most programs to manage calendars and work schedules can also benefit from this approach. Applications that require a reliable and timely feed of information, e.g., stock market quotes, can also be improved by using a CDN.

The manner in which these (and some other) applications can be improved using CDNs is discussed at length in Chapter 7.

1.3.2 Applications Unsuitable for a CDN

Not all applications are good candidates for a CDN. Applications that involve a lot of updates to a shared piece of data are not quite appropriate for a CDN. For example, a single chat room instance where information from multiple sources needs to be combined in sequence is not very suitable for performance improvement using multiple surrogate servers. However, there are other ways to use a CDN in order to improve a commercial chat room service. If there are multiple discussion topics (each with their own distinct set of participants) available from a service provider, each of the discussion topics could be held at a different surrogate.

Applications that need concurrent access from multiple locations are not very suitable for a CDN. Thus, access to a shared department database to which updates are frequently made may not be possible in a CDN. Applications that require strong transactional semantics are not very well suited for a CDN. Although distributed transactions are indeed possible, it is often more efficient to have a transaction performed only at a single site. Thus, a CDN may not be the best match for improving the performance of a banking system.

Applications that have strong security needs are not good candidates for a CDN. It is possible to process credit cards at the surrogates, but the surrogates need to be trusted and secure. In general, it is easier to build a single secure site (e.g., at the main server) than to maintain good security at multiple, geographically distributed surrogates. Therefore, trusted and secure data may not be the best candidate to place on a surrogate. Security, unfortunately, always comes at the expense of performance. However, depending on the security level of the surrogates, it may be possible to place a limited amount of secure content on a surrogate.

Despite these limitations, a large number of applications are very well suited to a CDN approach. Many applications contain a mix of functions that can be off-loaded to a surrogate server and those that cannot be off-loaded. Such applications can still benefit from the use of CDNs to improve some aspects of their performance. For example, a web-based store can be considered as an application offering two functions—browsing and buying. Browsing refers to functions needed by a web user to search through a catalogue and select items that she or he may be interested in buying. "Buying" refers to functions needed for the actual purchase, e.g., processing credit cards. In this application, the browsing functions can be off-loaded to a surrogate and the buying functions are probably best kept at the main server. Since most web stores experience considerably larger amounts of browsing that buying, such an off-load is likely to result in significant improvements in the store's customer-perceived performance.

1.4   ENVIRONMENTS FOR CONTENT DISTRIBUTION NETWORKS

In this section, we take a look at some of the operating environments in which content distribution networks may be used effectively. Although the basic technology used for CDNs across the environment will be the same, each operating environment provides a different level of administrative control and varying security levels for the surrogate servers. Therefore, the operating environment has a significant influence on the type of solutions one can use to build a CDN, as well as the type of functions that can be off-loaded to a CDN.

The three types of environments that we consider are those of an enterprise, a Internet service provider (ISP), and the public Internet. We assume that all the networks are based on IP technology, and the primary difference between them is in how they are administered.

The enterprise environment refers to the networks found in

large corporations such as IBM, Intel, or General Electric. These corporations typically have several branches located at multiple campuses. The typical network configuration consists of several campus networks connected together by a backbone network. The backbone network typically consists of leased lines obtained by the enterprise from a telecommunications company or an ISP. In general, campus networks operate at much higher speeds than the backbone network.

The enterprise campuses are often connected via an access router to one or more ISPs. An ISP may support multiple enterprises, each of which connect to it by means of an access router. From the perspective of the ISP , the network consists of several access routers connecting it to its customers, and another group of routers (which we will refer to as core routers) that connect the access routers together. All the core routers and access routers are within the administrative control of the ISP. In addition to the access router which connects an ISP to its enterprise customers, some ISPs may have locations where individual customers can dial into the network in order to access the network. These locations define the points of presence (POPs) of an ISP. A POP may support access by means of routers, by means of dial-in lines, or both.

ISPs typically interconnect with other ISPs at selected locations. These locations are known variously as Internet exchange points (IXPs), network access points (NAPs), metropolitan area exchanges (MAEs), or federal Internet exchanges (FIXs). Such exchange points may connect a regional ISP to a national ISP or act as a conduit among several different ISPs. ISPs would typically have peering agreements among themselves as to what type of traffic they will accept from other ISPs at an exchange point.

The conglomeration of all the different ISPs in the world is the public Internet. It consists of the network formed by the interconnection of all the ISPs at exchange points. Unlike the enterprise or ISP networks, the Internet does not have a single administrative authority.

1.4.1 CDNs for an Enterprise Environment

The typical enterprise application is hosted at one of the campuses and accessed by users all across the enterprise. If a user's campus has good connectivity to the hosting campus, performance is typically good. However, if the connectivity of the user to the hosting campus is through a congested backbone link, the perceived performance can be quite erratic. As an example, consider a company that hosts a directory of all employees at a site in the United States. Most of the campuses within the United States have good connectivity with the hosting campus, and the performance of the application is quite acceptable. However, users at sites in Europe and Asia may not be quite happy at the performance of the system.

Within an enterprise, some applications can benefit tremendously from the use of CDNs. If surrogate servers are available at each of the different campuses, users are likely to have a relatively good connection to one of the surrogates. Applications that are used across multiple campuses can benefit from the performance improvement available due to the presence of these surrogates. If the bottlenecks within the network are known, one can place surrogates to work around such bottlenecks without placing a surrogate at each of the campuses. Considering the example of the directory application mentioned earlier, surrogate servers may be placed in Europe and Asia to improve the response time experienced by users at those locations. The surrogate server in Europe will handle all requests from all the campuses in Europe.

An enterprise has administrative control over all the applications that are installed within its network. These include applications that are needed for operation of the network, e.g., the domain name server or the routing daemons. The enterprise can control the configuration of existing applications to exploit the presence of surrogates at various sites. If the enterprise is developing a new application, or is creating a new version of an existing application, it can modify the design to exploit the capabilities of a content distribution network. An enterprise has complete control over how to operate and exploit a content distribution network for its internal applications.

The enterprise must weigh the potential improvements in service against the cost of operating and managing the surrogates that are distributed across multiple campuses. Most enterprises tend to centralize their operations and application support at single sites in order to reduce the costs associated with managing the servers and applications. In order for the content distribution approach to become feasible within the enterprise, the surrogate

servers must be designed to be very easy to manage and administer.

1.4.2 CDNs for an ISP Environment

An ISP typically provides network-level connectivity to its customers. In this role, the ISP does not have control over the types
of applications that are communicating across its network. However, it does have control over the configuration of the routing
protocols and any servers needed to run the network itself.

For an ISP offering only network-level connectivity to its customers, the notion of content distribution networks is not very relevant. However, many ISPs provide more than simple network-
level connectivity to their customers. For many common types of
applications, an ISP may provide surrogates. The application surrogates can help in reducing the application response time, as
well as the bandwidth that needs to be carried across an ISP network. Some of the surrogates may provide other functions, e.g.,
protecting against spammed mail or filtering out objectionable
content.

For example, many ISPs provide proxies for web servers. These
proxies can implement functions such as caching of static images
and static content, transforming the pages, or filtering out objectionable content using the PICS [16] rating scheme. Such a proxy
may be implemented in a transparent manner such that a client
is unaware of its presence. Each proxy can be used as a surrogate
server. An ISP may combine the collection of proxy servers it supports at its POPs in order to deliver a CDN solution to its customers. An ISP may want to restrict the type of applications it
supports on its surrogate servers. Most ISPs would tend to support common applications, e.g., file transfer, mail servers, web
servers, etc. at the surrogate servers, as opposed to supporting
any generic applications at the surrogate sites.

The advantage of an ISP offering the content distribution solution is that it is a relatively inexpensive effort (compared to an enterprise or a content distribution service provider). Most ISPs already have several POPs located at various geographic locations,
and it is a relatively easy effort for them to offer a content distribution solution using the preexisting proxies at these POPs. The
ISP would still incur the costs involved in managing and operating the different surrogate sites.

1.4.3   Content Distribution Service Providers

Although ISPs or large enterprises have the administrative control and facilities available to operate a content distribution network, they are not the only players in the field. The initial phase of content distribution offerings within the Internet is characterized by many third-party suppliers that offer content distribution services for other sites. The content distribution service provider (CDSP) is an organization that operates a large number of surrogates at various locations throughout the Internet. The customers of the service provider are other organizations hosting their applications over the Internet.

Like the ISP, the CDSP does not have control over the application deployed by its cutomers. Therefore, the CDSP needs to choose a set of applications that would be supported at the surrogates for its customers. The most common applications supported by such CDSPs are web servers and multimedia (audio/video) servers. For web servers, many CDSP offer a service that allows the downloading of embedded images from a surrogate rather than from the original web server.

Since the CDSP does not have control over the network routing tables, the mechanisms used by a CDSP to direct requests to its surrogate servers tends to be more limited than the ones an ISP can use. However, with some support from its customers, this problem can be worked around fairly easily. A summary of the techniques that can be used by a CDSP can be found in Chapter 3.

The CDSP has a strong factor in its favor. As mentioned earlier, the major concerns regarding the use of content distribution networks are issues related to management and operation of the surrogate servers. The CDSP off-loads the burden of this management from its customers, and allows its set of surrogate servers to be used by customers, who in turn find it much easier to develop and deploy applications for a CDN.

1.5   THE COMPONENTS OF A CONTENT DISTRIBUTION NETWORK

Having explored the background and environment related to content distribution networks, let us look at the inner workings of content distribution networks. We will take a look at the different operational components that make up a CDN.

Since the primary goal of a CDN is to improve the scalability and performance of an application, the different sites that make up a CDN should be designed for scalability. This includes the various surrogate sites as well as the original site, which must be designed to support access by a large number of client users. Thus, the first component of a CDN is a scalable site design. Scalable site design includes the various methods that allow a site to support more clients than a single server machine would.

Each CDN consists of multiple surrogate sites and an original site. Each of the surrogate sites and the original site may consist of a single machine or a large cluster of machines designed using a scalable site design technique. Due to the costs involved in installing and maintaining a large site, it follows that there are two common types of CDN solutions—(i) one can have a large number of surrogate sites that are single machines or (ii) one can have a small number of surrogate sites that consist of a cluster of machines. The surrogate site administration issues related to each of these scenarios are slightly different. It is also possible to have a CDN with tiers, in which a CDSP with a large number of simple surrogate sites utilizes the services of another CDSP with a set of small (but scalable cluster sites) surrogate sites that provides its services to the origin site.

The next component of a CDN solution is the technique used to route the clients/users of an application to one of the surrogate sites instead of the origin site. Such a routing may be achieved by a variety of techniques, using the features of network directory services, network routing tricks, or modifications to the application. Depending on the environment within which a CDN is deployed (i.e., the Enterprise, ISP, or CDSP), one or more of these techniques will be better suited to the task of routing clients to the surrogate server. The client routing scheme is the second component of a CDN.

In order to achieve the performance gains that are the focus of a CDN solution, each client must be routed to a surrogate server that is located close to it. Making this determination implies that each CDN should maintain a routing table mapping various clients to a surrogate server site; this routing table should be modified according to the current load on the network and the surrogate server sites. We refer to this task as network performance estimation, and it is the third basic component of any CDN solution.

Since each surrogate server acts like an enhanced cache for the data/application logic that is stored at the origin server, the fourth component of a CDN consists of the techniques that are used for managing cache coherency and consistency among the different surrogate server sites and the original server site.

The various surrogate server sites and the origin server form an overlay network that is superimposed on the normal network connecting the clients to members of this overlay network. The networking infrastructure between the surrogate server sites and the origin servers is the fifth component of a CDN. The infrastructure must also incorporate support for managing the geographically distributed CDN sites.

In each of the following chapters, we look more closely at each of these components in more detail. This examination is followed by a chapter that describes how these components can be combined together to provide a CDN-based solution for a variety of applications.

2 Site Design and Scalability Issues in Content Distribution Networks

Each content distribution network (CDN) consists of a number of sites, with each site containing one or more machines. These sites may include the origin site as well as several surrogate sites. Since the eventual goal of CDNs is to provide support for applications that are accessed by a large number of users, each of the sites must be designed to be scalable and resilient when faced with a large number of users.

Some of the sites used as surrogate sites or origin sites may consist only of a single machine. In this case, the machine must be chosen to be fast enough to meet the number of users that are expected at the site. However, in many instances, the total number of users can exceed the amount that can be handled by the fastest available machine without a noticeable degradation in performance. In this case, multiple machines are needed to service these requests. In this chapter, we look at the different techniques that can be employed to use more than one machine to develop a more scalable site.

In a sense, a CDN is also a technique allowing use of many machines to provide a scalable solution for hosting applications. The only difference is that the different machines making up a CDN are (or may be) located at sites that may be geographically distant and typically connected over a wide area network. In contrast, a single site will contain many machines that are physically close to each other and interconnected by a local area network. It follows that some of the techniques used for building a scalable site using multiple machines can also be used when some of the machines are separated by a wide area network. However, the characteristics of the wide area network differ significantly from the characteristics of a local area network. A wide area network has large round-trip latencies and typically less bandwidth and is more susceptible to congestion. As a result, the performance characteristics of the same scheme could be quite different depending on whether it was used in a wide or local area network.

It should to be noted that scalable site design techniques will be adequate to meet the performance and scalability needs of any application if the network interconnecting the clients and servers is sufficiently fast. As technology improves, it may be possible in some situations to have a network that is comprised of fast links that never run out of capacity. In the presence of a network with good and predictable performance characteristics, a scalable site is sufficient for providing a good response time to the users. However, there are many environments in which the network's performance is unpredictable or poor. An example would be the network connecting the U.S. branch of a large corporation to its overseas branch in Asia. This link is likely to have a much larger round-trip delay and less bandwidth than a local area network. Another example is the Internet, in which performance is unpredictable due to varying traffic loads. In these cases, a scalable site design should be coupled with CDN techniques in order to achieve good performance for the end user.

The next section of this chapter provides a brief overview on how clients communicate with servers within the network. This is followed by a section that discusses the different techniques that can be used to combine multiple machines to provide a more scalable solution, and a section in which we show how these solutions can be used to develop a scalable site for hosting high-volume web servers. Although the examples concentrate on web-based applications, it should be noted that similar techniques can be used for other applications on an IP network, and for applications using networking protocols other than IP as well.

2.1 COMMUNICATION IN COMPUTER NETWORKS

When two applications communicate on a computer network, one plays a passive role and the other plays a more active role in establishing the communication. The one in the passive role is typically referred to as the server, and the one in the active role is typically referred to as the client. The server application waits for clients to establish a connection with it. The client application must find the server and send a message indicating that it wants to connect with it. After the server responds to the client and a specific set of handshake messages are exchanged, the two applications can exchange data with each other. The details of the handshake depends on the specific communication protocol used.

In order to initiate the first message to the server, the client needs to identify the server in some manner. This identification includes two parts; the first part identifies the machine on which the server application is running, and the second part identifies the application on the machine (there may be more than one server application on the same machine). The part identifying the machine is the one we will focus on here. The common paradigm used in most network architectures is that each machine in the network be given a unique name. The name is usually chosen to be something suitable for the needs of the users of the network. In addition to the machine name, each machine has one or more network addresses. The network address is an identifier that is selected to make the operations of the network efficient.

As an example, let us consider the TCP/IP protocol suite [21]. Within this protocol, each machine is given a machine name (known as the fully qualified domain name) that is a long human-readable string of characters identifying the machine. The network address (called the IP address) is a 32-bit-long integer, with each interface on a machine being associated with an IP address. As another example, the ATM protocol uses a hierarchically structured network address that looks like a telephone number (E.164 style address). When LANs are interconnected over an ATM infrastructure using LAN emulation, (i.e., when LAN interfaces are users of the ATM network), the MAC addresses of the interfaces connected to the ATM network are the machine names [10]. The machine name is the identifier expressed according to the needs of the users of the network, and the network address is the identifier expressed according to the needs of the network.

When the client attempts to talk to the server, it first maps the machine name to a network address. This is done by the client talking to some type of a directory server, which maintains the mapping of machine names to network addresses. The directory server for the TCP/IP protocol suite is known as the domain name service, wheras the directory server for LAN emulation over ATM is known as the LAN emulation server.

The mapping between machine names and network address

may be one-to-one or one-to-many, depending on the communication protocol. The TCP/IP protocol suite uses addresses to identify a network interface on a machine, so machines with multiple network interfaces can have more than one IP address, and a single machine name can map onto many network addresses. The typical mapping used in the LAN emulation over ATM is one-to-one.

2.2   SCALABLE SITE ARCHITECTURE

The design of a scalable site can essentially be defined as the problem of creating a server application that appears to be running on a single machine to the client, even though it consists of multiple server applications running on independent machines. When a client request comes into the site, it is handled by the application running on one of the independent machines. In this section, we look at the various techniques that can be used to make sure that the request is handled by one of the machines within the network.

The techniques described here can be divided into two main categories—the first one involves client participation and the second one does not. When client participation is involved, the client machine has to perform some actions in order to select an appropriate machine. Client participation is a good approach when it is possible to control both ends of a communicating application. If you are an application provider who is writing both the client and the server portions, client participation can increase the efficiency of load balancing. If you are a network operator within an enterprise, you can place surrogates at selected intranet locations in order to gain some control over the client side of a communication. However, in may cases, your control may only be on the server side of the communication. If you are operating a web server, you cannot control the type of browsers used to access your site. In those cases, only the techniques that do not require client-side participation would be applicable.

It must be kept in mind that running the server side of an application on multiple machines in parallel is difficult to do for all applications in general. However, a large class of server applications can be executed in parallel relatively easily. If a server application is stateless, i.e., it is capable of fulfilling each request from the client without requiring any information regarding how such requests were processed in the past, it can be run on parallel machines without a lot of work. A common instance of a stateless application is a read-only application, one that simply provides read-only access to some data, performing transformations like putting the data into a format comprehensible to the client. A web server serving static pages would fall within this category of applications. If the data being accessed is replicated consistently across several machines, such applications can be run concurrently on many parallel machines. An alternative is to have all the machines access a common shared store for the data. With a shared store, some applications that need state information, e.g., the outcome of a prior request, can also be run in parallel as long as the state is maintained in a shared store. In the rest of this chapter, we will assume that the applications running at the server site are ones that permit easy parallel execution on multiple machines.

2.2.1 Front-End Load Balancer

The use of a front-end load balancer before a set of servers is the most common technique to allow use of multiple machines while providing the illusion of a single system to the client. When a site is designed using a front-end load balancer, it has a configuration as shown in Figure 2.1. Clients communicate to the site using the external network. The access to the external network is via the load balancer that connects to multiple servers over a high-speed server LAN. There is a single machine address advertised for the entire site, and clients communicate to the server at the advertised machine address. Internally, the different machines may have the same or different machine addresses, depending on the needs of the specific network and transport protocols. Typically, the machine address advertised is that of the front-end load balancer. One nice thing about such a load balancer is that it can be introduced between an existing client and an existing server transparently, i.e., without the client or server machine being aware of the load balancer's existence.

On receiving each request from the client, the load balancer determines which of the several servers at the site should service the request. The request is then forwarded to that server. If a client is establishing connection to the site, the load balancer directs the client to one of the servers selected so as to cause a uniform distribution of traffic load. Once a client has been directed to a specific server, the load balancer creates some state information so that it

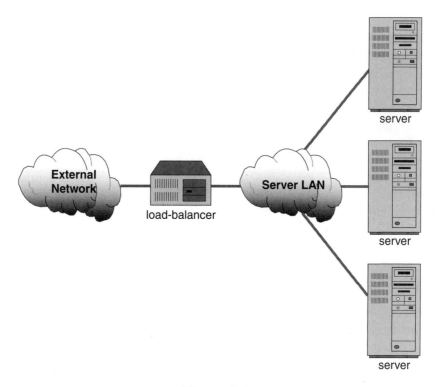

Figure 2.1.

can select the same server on subsequent packets/requests from the same client. For the reverse communication from servers to clients, the resulting packets may flow through the front-end load balancer, or they may be able to take a different path. The former would usually allow for a more efficient load balancer.

The load balancer software may make the distribution decision based on a number of different criteria. From the side of the servers, the criterion used is the traffic load among the different servers. Other information contained in a packet may be used to decide how to distribute a request. The amount of information used depends on the software contained within the load balancer. Some load balancers only look at transport and network headers in order to make their distribution decisions, some look at application-level information to make a more informed decision, and others may implement a full-fledged application proxy inside of the load-balancer to make their decision.

The transparency property of the front-end load balancer makes it a very attractive solution for load balancing in a scalable site design. However, the front-end load balancer can become a single point of failure. The front end has to process all the requests coming into the site, and care needs to be exercised so that it does not become a performance bottleneck itself.

A more detailed description of the variety of load distribution schemes in the context of TCP/IP networks is provided in Section 2.3.

2.2.2 Broadcast and Filter

Another approach that can be used to direct requests to one of the many server machines is the broadcast and filter approach. In this approach, the request is simply sent to all of the servers that are present at the site, and a collaborative protocol is used among the different servers to ensure that only one of the servers actually processes that request. As an example of a simple collaboration protocol, each server may keep a list of client network addresses that it will accept. Requests from other clients are filtered out. If the set of client network addresses used by any two servers are disjoint and each client network address belongs to one of the servers, each client can be easily mapped to one of the servers.

The advantage of the broadcast and filter approach is that it does not require a special front-end processor and therefore avoids a single point of failure. Its main limitation is that the load distribution on different servers can be largely unbalanced. Although the load balancer can make attempts to distribute traffic to different servers so that they all have an equitable load, it is hard to come up with filter rules that will result in a balanced load on the servers using a broadcast and filter approach.

2.2.3 Smart Directory Server

Since most networking protocols incorporate the notion of a address as well as a machine name, it is possible to direct clients to different server machines during the translation from machine name to machine address. Before a client communicates with the server, it needs to perform a directory lookup to translate the machine name to a machine address. At this step, different clients can be provided with different machine addresses in order to direct them to the different server machines.

The nice thing about using a directory server is that it does not require a separate box in front of the different servers. The servers can thus be located in different locations, and the directory scheme can be used for a CDN as well as for a single site. However, in some cases, client applications skip the translation stage. The skipping of the translation stage may occur because the client may have cached a machine address provided in the past by a directory server, or the client might have been provided the machine address rather than the machine name of the server by a user.

Different networking protocols invoke the translation at different stages of the communication process. Within TCP/IP, the address translation happens using a series of domain name servers prior to an actual connection establishment by the client. Within LANE over ATM, the translation is similarly done prior to establishing a virtual circuit for communication. In some other network architectures, e.g., in the IBM NBBS [17] architecture, a call is made to the directory service at the server end when the connection establishment request is received. Such a late binding provides some more flexibility in directing clients to one among many different server machines.

2.2.4   Smart Selection by Client

If we are in a position to influence the behavior of the client application, some of the onus of selecting the right server can be moved onto the client. Within this paradigm, the client will be provided the set of the possible servers that it can use for its communication. The client can then select one of the many servers that it finds suitable for its communication needs.

A selection of the right server by the client is an established practice in many types of client applications in order to guard against the failure of individual server machines. A domain name service client, for example, is usually configured with the identity of two or three domain name servers, and it selects the first available one on the list. Mail servers based on SMTP [18] similarly allow the configuration of more than one machines that can be used to send out outgoing mail.

The scheme can be extended to enable a client to select one out of several possible servers. This selection can be made either at the stage at which the directory server is used to translate the machine names to network addresses, or at the stage at which actual communication is established.

When a selection is made at the stage at which the name to address translation occurs, the directory server simply needs to return the network addresses of all the servers available at a scalable site. The client can then choose among them in a random fashion or in a round-robin manner.

When a selection is made at the time when communication is established, the client sends a request that is received by all of the servers at the site. Each of the servers respond to the request from the client, and the client selects one of the responding servers for further communication. As an example, the client will perform the actual communication with the server that is the first one to respond. The connection establishment process is aborted for all of the other servers. Such an abort will happen automatically in most communication establishment protocols if the client does not respond, or if the client sends an explicit message to terminate the process.

2.2.5 Client Redirection Protocol

When the client is the entity making the selection of the server, the servers have to rely on the behavior of the client in order to make the correct choice for the server. If the client machines are not fully secure, a malicious or malfunctioning client can easily misuse the scheme, resulting in unbalanced loads on the different server machines.

One alternative that allows the server site to take control of the decision is to have a redirection protocol with the client. When the client sends a message to the site for establishing communication, a machine at the site selects one of the many servers to whom the client ought to be redirected. The client is then told to contact the selected server to proceed with further communication.

Such a redirection scheme is available within the HTTP [19] protocol, although it can be designed at other layers of the protocol suite as well.

2.2.6 Concurrent Parallel Access by Client

Another option that is available to a smart client is to maintain communication with more than one server concurrently. In this

scheme, it is assumed that the client needs to make many requests to the server during the different stages of communication.
When the client receives information about the multiple servers
that are available at a site, it issues a request to each of those
servers. As the requests get completed, the client sends the next
request to the same server. Servers that are lightly loaded and
can respond to the client quickly get a larger share of the requests
from the client, and servers that are slow to respond get fewer requests. If all of the clients use such a concurrent parallel access
scheme, the load on the servers can be balanced out.

Depending on the nature and performance needs of the network, one can combined one or more of the techniques described
above to come up with a solution that can be used to design a
highly scalable site. In the next section, we look at how the different schemes can be used in the context of web hosting over a
TCP/IP network.

2.3   SCALABLE WEB SERVER SITE ARCHITECTURES

In many cases, one needs to deploy a website that will host a high
hit rate and a large number of concurrent requests. The concepts
outlined in Section 2.2 can be used to design a scalable site. Here
we take a look at the different ways in which they can be applied
to develop a scalable website architecture.

The simplest solution to a scalable website design is to use a
very fast machine that is adequate for handling the largest possible load that can be anticipated on the system. If it is possible to
find a fast enough computer that fits within the financial budget
for the project, using that machine would be the simplest approach. At sites in which budgetary concerns are not of primary
concern, multinode supercomputers are used to host websites and
web servers. At the time of writing this book, high-end IBM SP
[20] clusters can easily handle hit rates of over 4 billion web requests per day. Unfortunately, such servers are relatively expensive. Thus, other options that provide for a lower-cost solution
need to be explored. It should be pointed out that the high-end supercomputers are composed of many parallel processors, and their
hardware/operating systems provide the functions of load balancing and data consistency. In some sense, the scalability solutions
described in this section parallel the techniques used within the

supercomputers. However, since the data consistency needs of a web-based application are much less stringent than that of a general purpose operating system, solutions that are not appropriate for use within a supercomputer can also be used effectively.

For illustrating the different techniques as they are used in the context of web servers, we assume that we are designing the site for a company that is available at the URL http://www.company.com. We will also assume that this site requires three machines in order to meet its anticipated demand, and that the three machines are called A, B, and C. We also assume that the company has been allowed to use a class C address of 200.0.0.0, i.e., it can legitimately use any address in the range of 200.0.0.0 and 200.0.0.255 on the Internet.

While discussing the different options available for a scalable website design, I would like to remind the reader about the way in which HTTP works over TCP/IP. In any web transaction, the browser initially contacts the domain name server to map a host name at an IP address. The browser then requests a connection establishment to the specified IP address. The standard TCP connection establishment mechanism is a three-way handshake. It requires the client to connect to the server by sending a TCP segment in which the SYN bit is set (SYN and ACK are one-bit flags in the TCP segment header). The server then responds with a TCP segment that has the SYN and ACK bits set. The client then acknowledges the response from the server by sending another TCP segment with the ACK bit set. In this exchange, the TCP stacks on the client and server randomly generate and negotiate sequence numbers that are needed for reliable ordered data delivery. One important point to note is that the first two segments (SYN from the client and SYN-ACK from the server) being exchanged carry no data specific to the HTTP header. It is only on the third message (the ACK from the client) that the HTTP header that contains details of the specific URL being accessed by the client is made known to the server. More details on the TCP and HTTP protocol can be found in the book by Comer [21].

2.3.1 Front-End Load Balancers

The first solution to the scalable website design that we consider is the one that uses a front-end load balander. However, there are many ways in which a front-end load balancer can be used to for a scalable web-server. The front-end load balancer may act like a web surrogate for the site, or it may only act as a relay that forwards packets to one of the many servers at the back end.

2.3.1.1 *Surrogate Server Implementations*

When used as a surrogate, the front-end load balancer is the machine that corresponds to the global name of machine www.company.com. The real web servers, A, B, and C, are assigned other IP addresses available to the company. An example configuration that can be used for such a website is shown in Figure 2.2. We assume that the company has decided to publish the IP address of 200.0.0.129 as its well-known external IP address. In other words, the company will advertise to the Internet domain name service that the machine name www.company.com maps onto the IP address of 200.0.0.129. For the real web servers, which are shown in the figure as A.company.com, B.company.com, and C.company.com, the organization has decided to use

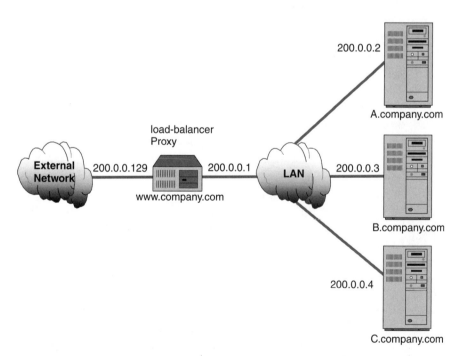

Figure 2.2.

the IP addresses 200.0.0.2, 200.0.0.3, and 200.0.0.4 respectively. The load balancer connects to machines A, B, and C via a subnet, and the IP address of the interface connected to the subnet is 200.0.0.1. The IP addresses are shown for ease in discussion, and other sets of IP address may be used with the same results. The mapping between the domain names of the IP address of the individual web servers, A, B, and C, may be advertised to the public domain name system, or the organization may choose to keep the mapping private.

When a client wishes to connect to the website of the organization, it queries the Internet domain name system to determine the right IP address of www.company.com. The client is provided the IP address of 200.0.0.129 and connects to the front-end load balancer. The load balancer accepts the connection, after which the client completes the TCP handshake and provides the URL of the resource being accessed at the site. At this point, the surrogate can decide which of the three web servers, A, B, or C, ought to be servicing this request. It establishes a separate TCP connection to the selected web server and relays the request to it for servicing. The load balancer then copies any data that it receives from the client to the selected web server and vice versa.

When used as a surrogate server, the load balancer has the maximum flexibility in determining how to direct the clients to different users. It can decide to route clients on the basis of the contents they are using, e.g., all images may be served from web server A, whereas all audio files are served from web server B. It can also route connections on the basis of the cookies placed on a client's browser. This will help in ensuring that connections from a client stick to a server (see Section 2.3.1.5). The load balancer can be interposed transparently before any type of web server and any type of client. However, this type of load balancer is also fairly inefficient. The load balancer has to service connections at the combined rate of all the web servers so as not to become a bottleneck.

It is worthwhile pointing out that the load balancer in a surrogate mode acts like a client to all of the servers within a network farm. Although the surrogate would typically behave like a standard client, it can also be enhanced to use a specialized protocol between itself and the servers. Therefore, a surrogate load balancer can also utilize any of the schemes described in Section 2.3.2 for load balancing.

2.3.1.1.1 Performance Optimizations for
Load Balancing Surrogates

There are different types of techniques that can be used to speed up the performance of a surrogate load-balancer. In software development, the easiest way to develop a surrogate is on top of a general purpose operating system, such as a Unix variant (Linux, Solaris, AIX, etc.) or Windows 2000. In such an implementation, a major performance bottleneck comes from crossing the system call boundaries. Most operating systems have a logical separation between operating system functions (which form the kernel of the operating system), and the functions provided by the application layer. In order to prevent a misbehaving application from crashing the entire system, most operating systems make the kernel functions available only via a set of system calls. These system calls perform a variety of checks to ensure that the call provided by an application will not cause the system to crash. Unfortunately, making these checks also implies that crossing the system call boundary is a slow process. When the load balancer has to relay a lot of data back and forth between the connections, the system call overhead penalty is being paid too many times.

In order to avoid this bottleneck, one can adopt one of two techniques:

1. Implement the surrogate load balancing function as a kernel routine
2. Try to split the functions between the application level and the kernel so as to eliminate the system call overhead in data transfer

One can implement a small HTTP surrogate server as a kernel function in any of the common operating systems. Such a surrogate server would be much more efficient than a surrogate server implemented in the application space. If you put serious effort into it, a web server can be implemented in really tiny systems [22]. When the web server is implemented in the kernel, there are no expensive system boundaries to cross and the load balancer can operate very efficiently. The same performance advantage can be gained by using an embedded operating system. Embedded operating systems (also known as real-time operating systems) are operating systems focused for small devices, e.g., television controllers or network routers. These devices are generally for a single purpose, and thus do not implement the strong insulation between the application level and kernel level functions. Surrogate load balacing functions implemented on an embedded operating system can result in a very efficient load balancer.

One of the ways to speed up the performance of a surrogate load balancer is to use a splicing approach to TCP connections [23]. The splicing approach works on the principle that the bulk of operations done by a surrogate load balancer consist of relaying data back and forth across two connections—one connecting it to the client, and the other connecting it to one of the back-end servers. Since the surrogate does not modify the packets being relayed back and forth, it only needs to do application level processing when the connection is established and the right server to process the request is determined. After the connection is established, the surrogate load balancer can transport the packets back to the original client, doing the minimum possible processing to maintain the illusion that the packets are flowing on the same connection that was established by the client to the surrogate. In order to do so, the surrogate needs to change the TCP and IP headers in the packets. The IP layer addresses have to be changed to make them appear to come from the surrogate. Thus, a packet traveling back from web server A to the client via the surrogate would require that the source IP address be changed from 200.0.0.2 to 200.0.0.129. On the reverse path, the destination address will be changed from 200.0.0.129 to 200.0.0.2. As mentioned earlier, when a TCP connection is established, sequence numbers are negotiated randomly. Thus, the sequence numbers need to be remapped to account for the difference between the initial sequence numbers used on the two spliced connections. Any change of these fields also requires checksum entries in the TCP and IP headers to be updated. However, the splicing approach can be implemented to obtain significant performance gains [23].

2.3.1.2 *Load Balancers Using Network*
Address Translation
An alternative way to implement a load balancer is to use a network address translator box as the front-end load balancer. Network address translation is a scheme of manipulating IP addresses of a packet so that packets coming from one machine appear to be coming from another machine. It has often been used as a way to handle the network address crunch that can arise if an organi-

zation has more machines than the set of legal addresses it has been allocated on the Internet.

The manner in which network address translation works is fairly simple. The network address translator box would be placed in front of all the servers, as in the configuration shown in Figure 2.2. The IP address assignment would be similar to that shown in Figure 2.2, and the external IP address (200.0.0.129) of the load balancer would be the externally advertised address of the site www.company.com. The packets from the external clients would be addressed to the load balancer. However, the load balancer does not accept any connections. Instead of doing the TCP processing, the load balancer selects one of the back-end web servers and forwards the packet to it. The transport protocol processing is done by the back-end web server.

The load balancer detects the start of a new connection by observing packets with the SYN flag turned on in the TCP header. It makes a load balancing decision, and creates an entry in a local table mapping the IP address of the client and the port number used for this new TCP connection to the selected web server. Subsequent packets from the client on the same connection are sent to the previously selected server. When an end of the connection is detected, as indicated by the presence of a TCP segment with the RST flag turned on, the entry is removed. The entry can also be removed if there is no activity on the connection for a long period.

When the back-end web server responds back to the client, it would generate packets with the IP address of the web server, e.g., web server A would generate packets that have the source IP address of 200.0.0.2. When the packet is actually delivered to the client, the packet needs to carry the source address of 200.0.0.129 (otherwise the TCP protocol at the client will get confused), so the packet needs to pass through a reverse network address translation phase.

The reverse network address translation can be done by the front-end load balancer, or it may be done by another network address translation device. The advantage of using a different network address translation device is that it reduces the amount of work the load balancer needs to do. In a typical web server farm, the number of packets flowing from the clients towards the servers are much less than the number of packets flowing from the servers toward the clients. This is to be expected since most web requests are small, whereas the resulting web pages downloaded from a server tend to be much larger. Thus, allowing the packets flowing from the servers to the clients to take a different path releases a significant amount of processor cycles to be used for load balancing. This allows for a more scalable solution. An alternative approach to using the network address translation is to have the address translation occur in the server itself. This can be done if the networking stack within the server has a module supporting network address translation, and it is configured to do the right translation.

The set of translation rules that need to be implemented for the configuration shown in Figure 2.2 to enable separate paths for packets to/from the server is shown in Figure 2.3. In this figure, I

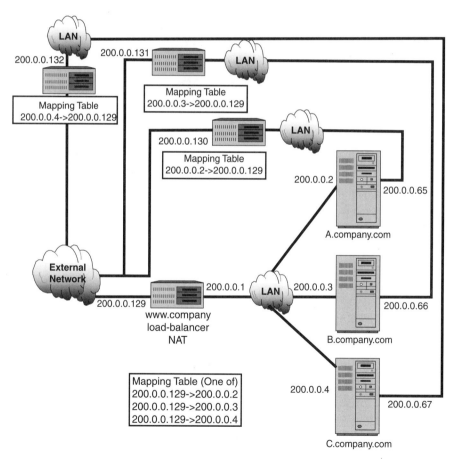

Figure 2.3.

have made the assumption that a different reverse network address translator will be used for each server. However, these three can be combined together, and their function performed by a single network address translator. The number of network address translators to be used for the forward or reverse path would be determined by the processing capacity of each of the servers and the boxes.

When operating on the same hardware, a load balancer implemented as a network address translator is likely to perform better than one implemented as a surrogate for several reasons:

1. There is no TCP processing to be performed at the load balancer

2. All of the packet manipulation takes place in the kernel

3. The reverse packets need not flow back through the same device

However, there is a downside to the use of load balancers at the network level only: their support of client stickiness is limited (see Section 2.3.1.4 for more details).

2.3.1.3 Shared IP Addresses

The load balancing solution presented in the previous section required a network address translation on the reverse path, i.e., on the packets that flow from the servers to the clients. This forces a website operator to choose between two approaches:

1. Use the same load balancer for the forward and reverse paths

2. Use one or more network address translation boxes on the reverse path

Both of these options have their drawbacks. The first requires the front-end load balancer to process a large number of packets, resulting in reduced efficiency. The second results in extra boxes, leading to additional costs in acquiring and managing/operating those boxes.

If we can develop a solution allowing all the web servers use the same IP address (the one advertised to the external DNS), the network address translation boxes on the reverse path can be eliminated. This would simplify the configuration of the web server farm as well as eliminate the need to process the packets on the reverse path.

If all the web servers have the same IP address, the front-end load balancer cannot use their IP address to distinguish between them. It must use some other identifier to distinguish among the different servers. One identifier that can be used is the MAC address of the interfaces connecting the servers and the load balancer. The load balancer uses a slight modification of normal IP processing to forward the packet. Once it has determined the right server to forward the packets to, it creates a MAC packet with the right address to ensure delivery of the packet. The back-end servers receive the packet, since it is addressed to their MAC address, check the IP address to see that the packet is intended for them, and then receive the packet for further processing. When they send the packet out, they send it out using the right IP address. The configuration of www.company.com site would be as shown in Figure 2.4. Note that many machine interfaces have the same IP address, the externally published address of 200.0.0.129. This is a somewhat nontraditional approach to assigning IP addresses that enables an efficient load balancing solution to be obtained.

Note that the use of a MAC address implies that the servers and the load balancer need to be on the same physical IP subnet. If the servers need to be placed on more than one subnet, one would need to create a hierarchy of dispatchers wherein each dispatcher performs the load balancing function for the other dispatchers (or servers) that are one level below it in the order. An alternative would be to use a physical layer protocol in which a larger number of machines can be placed on the same IP subnet. As an example, the number of machines that can be on an Ethernet LAN segment is typically less than the number of machines that can be on an ATM network.

In this configuration of the load balancer, it is not necessary for the load balancer to have the same IP address as that of the back-end server. As long as the routes in the network are established so that the front-end load balancer is the machine to receive the IP packets prior to the servers, this solution will work. The load balancer needs to detect the start of client requests (check for the SYN flag in TCP), and maintain a set of active connections and the servers they are being routed to.

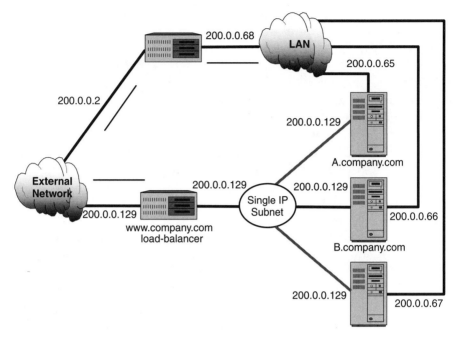

Figure 2.4.

Like other network-level load-balancing schemes, this approach also suffers from the stickiness issue described in the next section.

2.3.1.4 The Stickiness Issue in Load Balancing

When the load balancing task is performed, care has to be taken to ensure that a client is forwarded to the same server machine as much as possible. A client needs to be mapped to the same server on its subsequent visits. Once a client has been assigned to a server, it is highly desirable that the client remain with that server in subsequent requests. This is called "stickiness."

Stickiness is desirable because many websites maintain session state across multiple HTTP requests. Although the original web-based protocol was a stateless protocol, the need for tracking user activities has led to schemes that maintain some information across multiple web sessions. The most common example of this session state is the use of shopping carts at many e-tailer websites. We define an e-tailer as a site that is offering some products

---

MAC Addresses and IP Subnets

Packets in an IP network are forwarded to their destinations on the basis of IP subnets. An IP subnet is a set of IP addresses that are connected on the same physical network. A physical network could be a segment of a serial line, an Ethernet LAN, or an underlying ATM network. Just as IP addresses identify machines on the Internet, each physical medium has its own set of addresses (called MAC addresses) that identify the machines on it. A MAC address is only visible and usable by machines on the same physical network. When forwarding a packet, an IP device first checks to see if the destination is on the same IP subnet. If so, the device determines the MAC address to which it needs to be sent, and prepares the packet so that it can be delivered to the right address. If the destination is not on the same IP subnet the IP device will determine the best next IP machine on the same physical subnet, and send the packet to it for further delivery. There are limits on how many machines can be placed on each LAN segment without a loss in performance. These limits are determined by underlying network technology, with separate limits for Ethernet, token rings, and ATM networks.

---

or services for sale on the World Wide Web. Each request from the client to the server while searching through a catalogue or selecting an item to be placed in the shopping cart for purchase is an independent HTTP session. In order to be user-friendly, one wants to enable the client to intersperse HTTP sessions while searching through the catalogue and selecting items for purchase in any order, and allow a single final checkout of all the selected items. In order to enable this, the state of the shopping cart (the items the user has selected for purchase) needs to be remembered across multiple HTTP sessions.

There are three methods that are commonly used to track session information: use of browser cookies, URL rewriting, and shared session storage. Two of these approaches, namely browser cookies and URL rewriting, require some level of support for stickiness from the load balancer.

A cookie is a piece of data that web servers can place on a browser. A cookie may be stored by the browser on the disk of the client machine, or it may be stored only in memory. The cookie stored on disk by the browser will persist even if a user terminates the browser application. The cookie stored in memory is only available as long as the browser process is active. On each subsequent visit to the server, the cookie is sent back to the server. Cookies, however, have a maximum length limit of 4096 bytes, so the information contained within them is limited. As a result, many sites choose to simply store some type of index in the cookie, and use that index to look up a more detailed state description at the servers. Information such as a description of the different items selected for potential purchasing at an e-tailer site may not fit into the limited size available a cookie. The server will store the detailed state in some local storage. If this local storage is not shared by the other servers, it is important that the client stick with the server it visited the first time. Otherwise, the state information would be lost, and no e-tailing site would like to have the potential items to be purchased vanish suddenly from a user's shopping cart.

An alternative to cookies for keeping session state associated with clients is to use URL rewriting. Many users are apprehensive about enabling cookies in their browsers and disable this feature. The nice thing about URL rewriting is that it cannot be disabled easily by the user. However, whereas cookies can persist and thus be used to track the identity of a browser for an extended period, the lifetime of a rewritten URL is quite short.

URL rewriting relies on the fact that most people would tend to visit a first page, and then follow links in that page to other information at a site. When a user visits the site for a first time, e.g., to the site www.company.com, he is given a page in which all the embedded links that normally would be of the form www.company.com/link are changed to a format resembling www.company.com/uid/link. The uid part is a randomly generateed unique identifier associated with that user, and is ignored as far as serving pages to the user is concerned. As long as the user follows the links on the site, or performs searches using the links provided in that page, the uid field is carried in the requests and allows the site to match each request made previously by the same user. As long as the user does not type the original address of the index page, www.company.com, again, the uid field is preserved. Although this is not quite as persistent as the cookie, it has the advantage that the user cannot easily disable this session tracking. A determined user can, of course, find ways to parse the pages returned by the site and eliminate the sessions identifiers used by a specific site, but it is difficult to come up with a scheme that will work in a general environment. As with cookies, the uid field is small and often used to index a table stored at the server.

If the servers keep independent state tables on their local storage, a state created by one server has no meaning on another server. In this case, it is imperative that the client stick with the server they picked on their first visit. When a load balancer is implementing the full surrogate functionality on the front-end, implementing this sticky behavior is straightforward. The load balancer terminates the TCP connection, and performs the full HTTP processing of the request. The session state information, whether stored as a cookie or as a substring in the URL, is available to the load balancer. On each request, the load balancer checks to see if the session state information (cookie or URL field) is present. If it is not present, a server is selected and the response from the server monitored for the session state. This session state is entered into a session state table and the association with the selected server duly recorded. If a session state is found on the request, the session state table is checked to determine the appropriate server to forward the request to. If there is no matching entry in the session state table, the request is treated as if there were no session state.

As mentioned previously, the session state data is only available when the TCP connection is terminated at the load balancer. For the dispatchers that only look at packet header fields and do not terminate the TCP connection, it is not easy to determine the session state. The load balancing decision has to be taken at the time when the packet with the SYN flag turned on arrives at the load balancer. This packet does not carry the HTTP header (which includes the URL and the cookies), and so the network layer load balancer has no information to determine if the client is a repeat visitor who ought to be sent to another server. Every time a new TCP connection is established by the client, the load balancing decision needs to be made.

Some load balancers use a heuristic approach to solve this problem, e.g., remembering the IP address that connected in recent past, and remember the server used in the previous request. This approach would work well in a world in which each user had their own client workstation and a separate IP address. Although this is the norm in the current computing world, the client's IP address is often invisible to the server. This is due to the existence of proxies and security firewalls in the Internet. The server is then aware only of the surrogate's IP address instead of the client's IP address. As an example, most users of America On Line (the largest Internet service provider in United States) would access the Internet through one of a few proxies provided by America On Line. Similarly, most users at the IBM Watson Research Center access the Internet via a couple of SOCKS [24] servers at Watson. To any server on the Internet, the client IP address of two users coming from behind the Watson proxy appear to be coming from the same IP address (that of the SOCKS surrogate), and remembering the IP address of the client can lead to directing many requests to the same server, even if they were from different users.

An alternative approach that eliminates the stickiness problem is to maintain a shared store containing the session state for all the servers at the site. If the servers do not keep their own independent state tables, but rather keep them in a shared storage system, any server would be able to process the requests regardless of who handled the previous requests. Shared storage can be obtained by means of a dedicated storage server/file server that is used by all the servers. A simple way to obtain a shared storage server is for all the servers to mount the file system exported by the file server, and to keep the session state in this file system. Most operating systems provide support for exporting file systems over a network. As an example, the mount and export commands in Unix or the mapping of the network drivers in Windows operating systems can be used to achieve this goal.

2.3.1.5 *Load-Sensitive Balancing*

When web requests are being dispatched across different machines, the goal is to have all the back-end servers utilized equally. If the load on the servers is not equal (roughly), chances are that one of the more heavily utilized servers is providing a poor response time to the client requests. Clearly, this is a situation that ought to be avoided.

If all the back-end servers are identical, and all the web requests are similar in nature, then a simple round-robin selection of the servers is likely to result in an equitable load distribution on all the servers. However, in practice, the servers frequently differ in their configuration. A server may have a disk slightly slower than another, or may have a slightly different version of the operating system, or may have different amount of memory. Even when two systems are identical in hardware configuration, the allocation of files on the disks may follow a different layout, resulting in different performance for accessing the same page from the two systems. Similarly, different types of web requests impose different types of loads on the servers. Some web requests result in invocation of programs on the servers, others require a small file transfer, and others require the transfer of a large number of bytes. Thus, a simple round robin of requests among different users may result in an unbalanced load on the servers. Another cause of an unbalanced load would be clients sticking to a specific server. If a slightly higher percentage of active clients happen to stick to the same server, that server is likely to see an increased load level.

In order to guard against a possible unbalanced load, the front-end dispatcher needs to monitor the current utilization of each of the back-end servers, and direct more requests toward the servers that tend to have less utilization. In order to do so, the load balancer needs to periodically get a metric representing the utilization of the different back-end servers, and then use this metric when making load distribution decisions. If the probability of a new request going to the server is inversely proportional to the utilization metric of the server, the end result is likely to be an equitable load on all the servers.

The load balancer may use a variety of techniques to obtain the load on each of the servers. The load may be captured by simply retrieving the header of a chosen page at each of the servers, or by invoking a performance monitoring script at the server that can capture metrics like overall system processor utilization, number of active connections, etc. A load balancer would typically invoke a preconfigured URL at each of the back-end servers in order to invoke this script.

Regardless of the metric being measured by the load balancer, taking current utilization of servers into account is likely to result in a better overall response time from the combined system, a desirable attribute to have.

2.3.1.6　Fault Tolerance and Security Issues in
Load Balancing

When a front-end load balancer is used within a server farm, its failure could cause the entire site to become inaccessible, even though the servers at the site may still be operational. The only protection against failures currently known is redundancy. Thus, each site needs to plan for a backup load balancer that will automatically take over in case of the failure of the original load balancer.

The basic approach to fault tolerance is shown in Figure 2.5. The external network is connected to the site by at least two routers, each having its own access link. In case one of the access links fails, the other link would still provide connectivity. In case one of the routers fails, the other router would still provide connectivity. The routers are connected to at least two load balancers by a LAN. Each of the load balancers are connected to the servers (at least two) through another LAN. For extra reliability, even the LANs can be replicated. In this case, each of the routers/load balancers need to use a separate interface to connect with each such replicated LAN.

When every element in the system is replicated, the impact of a single failure is minimized. In case one of the elements fails, its redundant copy can take over. The redundant copy may operate as a stand-by, in which case it is only used when the original element fails. Another common approach is to use all copies of an element when they are available. When one element fails, the system continues to operate at a reduced capacity.

Hackers and malicious users are a reality in the Internet today, and are likely to be so for the foreseeable future. Thus, a server farm must provide adequate safeguards against potential attacks by malicious outsiders. On web server farms, safety is usually achieved by deploying one or more firewalls. The firewall allows only limited access to the various servers within the farm from different locations. For fault tolerance, each of these firewalls also ought to be replicated.

At least one set of firewalls is needed between the routers connecting the site to the external Internet and the load balancers. This set of firewalls will only permit the traffic addressed to the site's globally advertised IP address to reach the load-balancer. Depending on the nature of the load balancer, another set of firewalls may be needed to ensure that only the load balancers are

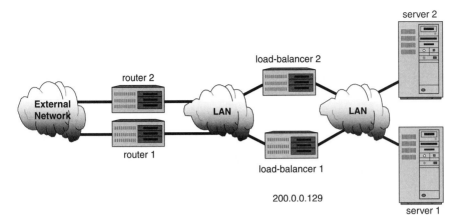

Figure 2.5.

sending packets toward the actual servers. Another set of fire-walls might be present between the servers and the external ac-cess routers for the outbound path in order to ensure that packets are flowing externally and only from selected ports within the server. A site may also have management consoles or special con-nections to other sites run by the same operator. These would re-quire their own set of firewalls.

2.3.2 Broadcast and Filter

The broadcast and filter approach provides an alternative ap-proach for multiple servers to work together without the need for a special front-end load balancer. This approach requires a special network protocol processing at each of the back-end servers, but the front-end load balancer can be replaced by a standard router with a minor configuration. This scheme relies on the fact that may LANs support a scheme that allows a packet to be broadcast to multiple receivers within the network.

When this approach is used, all the back-end servers use the same IP address, which is the one advertised externally. Each of the back-end servers receives a copy of every packet sent to the site. However, each server only accepts a subset of packets for fur-ther processing, and discards all the other packets. The rules for accepting packets need to be designed so that each potential client is mapped to exactly one of the back-end servers.

The trick to having all the servers receive a copy of the packets coming into the site is to configure the inbound router to have a static mapping between the publicized IP address and the MAC address that will broadcast a message to all of the back-end servers. Normally, routers discover the mapping between IP addresses and MAC addresses on an interface in a dynamic manner using the address resolution protocol (ARP). However, it is possible on most platforms to override this dynamic mapping with a statically defined mapping. In order to obtain scalability using this technique, it is sufficient that the externally visible IP address be statically mapped to a broadcast MAC address that reaches all of the backend servers.

Figure 2.6 shows one possible manner in which this technique can be used in the example we are considering. The external IP address of 200.0.0.129 is advertised for the site, and is routed through the access router as shown in the figure. The access router is configured to map this external IP address to a broadcast MAC address that includes the MAC addresses of the three servers. The three servers have filtering rules established such that (i) all clients with the IP address ending in the last two bits of 00 are mapped to server A, (ii) all IP addresses ending in the last two bits of 01 are mapped to server B, and (iii) all IP addresses ending with the last two bits of 10 or 11 are mapped to server C.

There are some nice properties of this solution. Since each client goes back to the same server, the stickiness issues do not arise at all. There is no load balancer, and no need for an address translation, so fewer boxes are needed at the site. However, the solution is also relatively inefficient. Since each server has to receive all the packets coming into the site, the servers needs to spend cycles deciding whether to discard or process a packet. For all discarded packets, this is a wasted effort. As a result, the servers are able to handle less traffic than they would if a front-end load balancer were being used.

2.3.3   Smart Directory Server

Since the IP protocol requires that a domain name such as www.company.com be resolved to an IP address prior to actual communication, one can use the translation stage to direct clients to different machines.

In order to understand how these solutions work, let us take a

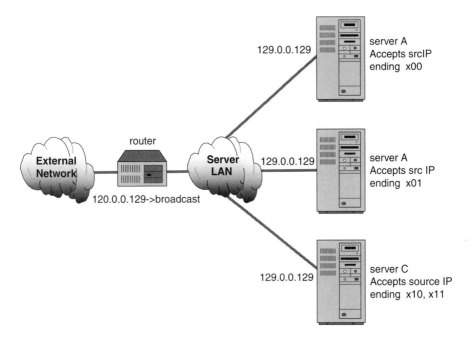

Figure 2.6.

quick look at the operation of the domain name system (DNS) in the IP network. Each domain name is a set of strings separated by dots; the first string is the machine name and each dot marks the beginning of a DNS domain. Thus, www.company.com is a machine named www in the domain company.com, which is part of the larger domain of .com. The process of domain name translation is provided by a number of "domain name servers." Each domain would typically have one name server that is considered the authentic source for providing names for address translation for that domain. The name servers are connected in a tree-like structure following a parent–child relationship that parallels the structure of the domain names. Thus, the domain name server for company.com would consider the domain name server of .com as its parent name server. Each name server knows the identity of its parent, and all of its children.

A client machine needing to resolve a name would go to a local name server. The name server may be the authentic name server of the local domain or another copy of it. If the name server does not have the information to provide the translation, it would forward the request to its parent. The parent name server would then decide to either forward the request to its child or, further up, to its parent, the decision being made by comparing the name being resolved to the domain of the name server. When a response comes back, the resolution is cached by the name servers for subsequent requests.

Normally, the requests carry the translation of IP addresses. There may be multiple IP addresses as a result of a translation. The authentic name server may also inform the requesting name server that the name being requested is an alias for another name. The working assumption is that each machine would have one primary or canonical name. If another alias name for the machine is being resolved, the canonical name can be returned. The use of canonical names increases the chances for a cache hit in the name resolution process.

There are at least three variants of the DNS-based schemes that can be used to distribute traffic to different machines.

In the first variation, the name server simply maintains all the public IP addresses associated with a domain name. The client is then expected to use one of these names to initiate the connection. The name server can swap the order in which it sends the IP addresses around for different requests. A client would typically pick the first IP address in the list to communicate, so different clients will be directed to different servers.

In the second variant, the site advertises a single domain name to the outside Internet. Let us assume that the name advertised in this manner is www.company.com. The site also uses one valid IP address per server on the Internet. Let us assume that the three addresses being used are 200.0.0.129, 200.0.0.130, and 200.0.0.131. As clients request the translation of the name www.company.com to an IP address, the domain name server hands out only one of these three addresses. It also requests that other name servers disable caching for the resolution of the name www.company.com. Each name resolution response from a name server has a time to live (TTL) field that states how long the response information is valid for. This TTL field can be reduced to a small value in order to disable (or at least reduce) caching.

In the third variant, the site uses four domain names for the site. The first one (www.company.com) is the one published and used by the users. The other three represent the domain names of the individual servers—A.company.com, B.company.com, and C.company.com. Each of the three machines use three different IP addresses, namely 200.0.0.129, 200.0.0.130, and 200.0.0.131. When a query for the name www.company.com comes in, the domain name server sends a response stating that the name www.company.com is an alias for one of the other three names— A.company.com, B.company.com, or C.company.com. The name is then resolved to the appropriate IP address for communication. This is using the notion of canonical names in reverse, providing one of the aliases instead of the original canonical name. However, the scheme will work with existing name server implementations.

The primary issue in use any of these variants is that of loading all the different servers in a balanced manner. Because of caching at the various name servers in the entire DNS structure, there is no strong correlation between a request seen at the authentic domain name server for a site and the traffic to the site. Thus, it becomes hard to control how much traffic is directed at each of the servers using that solution. In the second and third approaches, caching is turned off. This forces each domain name resolution request to be directed to the authentic domain name server for a site, which can then try to balance the requests among different servers.

In the real Internet, even this approach provides only a coarse level of control over the balancing of the requests to the different sites. Many existing domain name server implementations will cache DNS requests for an extended period anyway, even if the authentic name server may set a very low TTL in its responses. This is because the basic assumption in the design of the DNS server was that the name-to-IP address changes are relatively infrequent.

Caching of name-to-address bindings is a desirable aspect of the domain name system. Disabling caching means that there will be a higher load on the DNS servers. Caching also results in a quicker response on the name resolution to the client. So disabling caching can significantly increase the latency experienced by the user in establishing a connection. Caching also has the advantage that it maintains the stickiness of the client to the same server, which, as discussed previously, is a useful feature to have in the web server context.

Any amount of caching, however, will result in an unbalanced load on the different servers at the site. This is because not all name servers generate equal amounts of load on the site. The name server of a popular ISP, e.g., America OnLine (AOL) in the United States, would generate a lot more requests than the name server of a small corporation. Thus, the IP address that happened by chance to be cached by the AOL name server will experience much more traffic, which can lead to different servers being utilized to varying degrees.

Due to these concerns, the use of directory name servers may not be the best method for distributing load among multiple local servers. However, this approach can be used to advantage in content distribution networks, as explained in the next chapter.

2.3.4   Content Modification

An alternative way to direct clients in web server farms is by modifying the content on the website. In the web server, users typically access a front-end page (or index page) at a site, and then click on the different links in order to access other parts of the site. It is possible to modify the links so that they point to different servers, and thus the traffic load generated by following these links is distributed across the different servers.

In order to implement this scheme in the example we are considering, the site needs to have the index page accessible at the externally known location of http://www.company.com. Each of the servers at the site also has an externally known domain name—A.company.com, B.company.com, and C.company.com. One of these servers may also double as www.company.com. The main page (let us say it is index.html) may contain some embedded images as links as well as some pointers for future references. Let us assume that index.html is as shown with two embedded images and one link contained inside it. Code Excerpt 2.1 shows the HTML code that can correspond to index.html. In order to use content rewriting, the servers maintain multiple versions of the code, one each for the three different servers. The rewritten excerpt for server A is shown in Code Excerpt 2.2. Note that although the excerpt shown changes all of the links in the page, it is possible to change only some of the links in the page. Similarly, the externally visible IP address of the server can be used to make this change rather than the domain name.

When the client receives the index.html page as shown in Code Excerpt 2.2, it retrieves the embedded links from server A instead of the original server. By deciding which of the three different versions of index.html is handed out to the clients, the site can distribute the load to the various servers.

Code Excerpt 2.1

```
<HTML>
    <BODY>
    <IMG src="/images/image1.gif?">
        - text of page
    <href link="/info.html">
            Click here for more information
    </href>
    <IMG src="/images/image2.gif">
    <BODY>
</HTML>
```

Although the modification of content as described above can be used to direct content to different servers, there are some drawbacks associated with this scheme. The first one is that the client needs to establish a new TCP connection to the server whose links are contained in the modified page. Most current browsers are able to reuse a connection to retrieve embedded images contained within a page. Thus, a client would only establish one connection to retrieve the page shown in Code Excerpt 2.1. However, it would need two connections to retrieve the page shown in Code Excerpt 2.2, one connection to www.company.com and the other to A.company.com. Creating a new connection adds to the user-perceived latency at the site.

Code Excerpt 2.2

```
<HTML>
    <BODY>
    <IMG src="http://A.company.com/images/image1.gif?">
```

```
            - text of page
    <href link="http://A.company.com /info.html">
            Click here for more information
    </href>
    <IMG src="http://A.company.com/images/image2.gif">
    <BODY>
</HTML>
```

Another problem associated with content modification is that users tend to remember some of the links, e.g., by storing them in a bookmark folder. If a user bookmarks one of the links to A.company.com, it will continue to return to that server even if B or C might be the better one at that time.

Despite these drawbacks, content rewriting does provide a method for effectively changing the information contained within a site so that it can be distributed. This requires that there be enough intelligence built into the site so as to determine which of the different versions of the file is to be dispatched on each client request.

2.3.5   Other Schemes for Web Server Farms

In addition to the schemes described above, there are some other approaches that can be used to direct loads across multiple web servers at a site. One of these schemes is to have the client select randomly, or in some other fashion, one of the many servers that it can use for its communication. This can be done by the client selecting a server from the list of all IP addresses returned by a server for that machine. Other heuristics can also be used by the client to determine the server it ought to select for this connection.

A smart client browser can retrieve pages in parallel from multiple page servers. The scheme utilizes the fact that a client can request specific bytes of a web page from a specific server. The scheme uses all the servers for parallel access, requesting transfers in units of say 4 Kbytes. The client would ask all three servers for 4 Kbytes of data, requesting the first server for bytes from 0–4 K, the second for bytes from 4 K–8 K, and the like. With n servers, the client can have $4n$ Kbytes of transfer in progress at a given time. When a server sends the 4 Kbytes, it is asked to send the next 4K byte of the page. Since servers that respond quickly are asked to send in more bytes, the scheme automatically obtains a balanced load on the servers. Its limitation is that it can only be used for static web pages, and not for pages that are composed dynamically by executing programs at the server. The latter category of pages is on the rise in the Internet.

3 Wide Area Client Redirection Mechanisms

3.1 INTRODUCTION

A content distribution network consists of many geographic sites, each of which may be constructed according to the architecture described in the previous chapter. In that chapter, we also looked at several techniques for directing clients to one of the many servers that are part of a site. In this chapter, we look at the problem of directing clients to one of the geographic sites themselves.

Some of the techniques described in the previous chapter for directing clients to one of the servers within a site, e.g., specialized directory servers, can also be used for distribution in wide area networks. Other such techniques, however, will cause substantial degradation in performance or reliability. Some schemes make sense only in a wide area context, e.g., anycast or wide area route manipulation. In this chapter, we examine the various schemes and discuss their relative merits and demerits.

As in the previous chapter, we will first look at the problem in a general network and then consider a specific application, namely a web server running on a TCP/IP network.

3.2 GENERIC WIDE AREA ROUTING MECHANISMS

The problem of wide area client routing can be explained by referring to Figure 3.1. It shows a content distribution network with several sites scattered throughout a wide area network. Each site is shown as a little cloud to emphasize the fact that they can use more than one server at that site. Clients attempt to access the services offered by an application hosted at the content distribution network. The clients can originate from anywhere within the network. Two such sets of clients are shown in the figure. Each client needs to be directed to one of the sites within the content

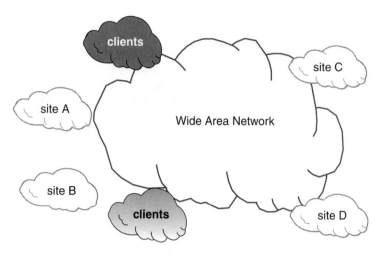

Figure 3.1.

distribution environment that is likely to provide the best performance for the client. As an example, one can assume that clients originating from the darker cloud area in Figure 3.1 need to be directed to site A, whereas the clients originating from the lighter cloud need to be directed to site B.

There are two questions that need to be addressed in this context:

1. How do we determine which of the sites is the most appropriate for the client
2. What mechanisms within the network can ensure that the client picks that site for communication.

I am deferring the solutions to the first problem to Chapter 4 and examine the second problem in this chapter.

We will assume that the generic network behaves in the same fashion as described in the previous chapter. Each server in the network is identified uniquely using a name. The clients uses a directory service to map the name of the server to a network address. The network address is used by the network to route packets sent by a machine to its appropriate destination. Clients would have a handshake with the server in order to begin communications and reliably transfer packets.

Each of the subsections below describes one of the schemes that can be used for client routing in wide area networks.

3.2.1 Extensions to Single Site Schemes

The first approach to wide area client routing is to simply extend the solutions that we discussed in the case of a single site. Some of these schemes would work well, whereas the other schemes may not work quite as well in the wide area environment.

In the previous chapter, we considered the following single-site schemes:

1. Front-end load balancer
2. Broadcast and filter
3. Smart selection by client
4. Smart directory server
5. A client redirection protocol and
6. Concurrent access by the clients.

Of these, the first three schemes have significant drawbacks in the context of wide area networks. The other four can be used in the wide area environment as well, but the last three would require modification of the client software.

The front-end load balancer (used as a reverse surrogate or otherwise) is one of the better solutions for distribution within a single site. To understand why this does not work as well in the wide area, let us consider the network shown in Figure 3.2. There would be only one front-end load balancer (assumed to be working as a surrogate) for all of the sites within the network. When the network is congested, some of the clients would not have good connectivity to the front-end load balancer. The goal of the content distribution network is to have this client be serviced by a surrogate site that has good connectivity to the client. However, in order to reach this surrogate site, the client needs to first go through the front-end load balancer, and that implies traversing the congested part of the network to the front-end load balancer. Since a well-connected surrogate is likely to be in the same part of the network where the client is located, chances are high that the surrogate site's connectivity to the load balancer is also congested. The entire communication path consists of four legs (as shown in

Figure 3.2) and all four legs are going through a congested area of the network. In this case, the better solution would be to just forgo all processing at the surrogate and do everything the the old fashioned way at the load balancer site. That would result in only two legs of the communication going through the congested part of the network and likely lead to better performance.

Note that using the front-end load balancer would have been a fine solution if the surrogate site were selected so that there was no congestion on the link between the surrogate site and the load balancer. This may indeed be true in some network configurations, e.g., when a surrogate site is closely located to the load balancer, or if a private high-speed network exists between the surrogate sites and the load balancer. In those cases, simply extending the single-site solutions would suffice for the purpose of improving performance.

One way to work around the four-leg congestion problem is to have only limited exchange with the front-end load balancer, e.g., just enough for the client to learn about the best surrogate site. This is the approach used in the client redirection protocol. Another approach would be to have the surrogate send data directly to the client instead of through the load balancer. This gives rise to the triangular route solution. Both of these solutions are discussed further later on in this chapter.

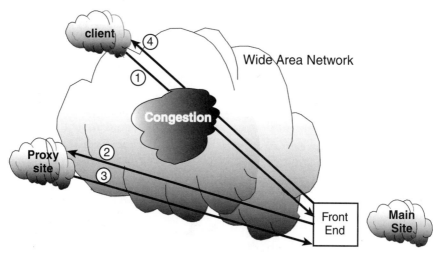

Figure 3.2.

The broadcast and filter approach also does not fare quite well in the context of the wide area network. In most of the networks of today, the wide area links tend to be more expensive and have less capacity than the local area networks. When a broadcast is being done to all of the servers within a single site, it is traversing a fast local LAN. Many LANs support broadcast natively, and even ones that do not can easily handle the extra packets that are generated in this fashion. Since the wide area tends to be composed of links with lower capacity, repeating packets on them causes unnecessary waste of precious bandwidth.

A smart selection from many servers within a single site is relatively easy for a smart client to do. Even a fairly simple scheme, e.g., selecting randomly from all of the available servers or selecting in some sort of round-robin fashion would result in a reasonably uniform load on the servers. However, in the context of the wide area environment, the client needs to incorporate another metric when deciding on which site is most appropriate, namely, the distance between each of the sites and itself. When the number of sites is large, communicating this information to the client can become quite complex.

The other solutions for the single-site scenario that may work reasonably well in wide area domain are considered in the next few subsections.

3.2.2 Triangular Routing

One approach to wide area load balancing that may work in some instances is the use of a front-end load balancer that does not sit along both the forward and reverse paths of the packet flow. One of the many sites is advertised as the primary site for the server. The clients are redirected to the other sites at the beginning of the connection. However, the response does not flow back through the primary site. The responses are sent back directly to the client by the selected site.

Figure 3.3 illustrates how the process operates. The inner cloud in the network is the region that is congested or performing poorly. The load balancer at the primary site has selected the site that is closer to the client. It forwards the packets received from the client to the surrogate site. The surrogate site sends the packets back to the client directly. Thus, the packets only traverse the

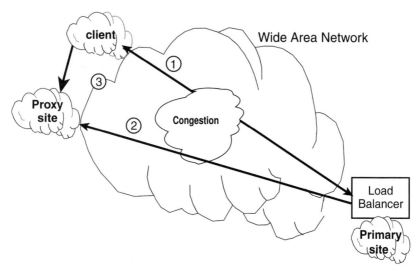

Figure 3.3.

congested part of the network in one round trip, no worse than in the original case.

One may question the need for the use of triangular routing in the case where content distribution is the primary solution being deployed in the network. As a long-term solution, it is much better to increase the capacity at the server site than to deploy a content distribution solution. However, triangular routing may work as a short-term solution for getting some extra processing capacity in a temperory manner.

3.2.3   Special Directory Servers

The approach of having a special directory server that can map a client to one of the many different sites can be used in the wide area network as well as in the single site. In this scheme, a special directory server is used to do the translation from the server name to a network address whenever a client wanted to communicate with the server. However, when used in the single site, the directory server simply had to consider the loads on the different servers in order to decide which one would be most appropriate for the client. In the wide area environment, the directory server has to take an additional factor into account, namely, the location of the client. It needs to select one of the sites that has good network connectivity to the client.

If the directory server knew the location of the client, it could probably choose the right site with a reasonable degree of accuracy. However, in some network protocols, the location of the client may not be known by the directory server. This can reduce the effectiveness of this scheme.

3.2.4 Client Redirection Protocol

A protocol that can be used between a client and a server to redirect the client to an appropriate surrogate site can be used to advantage in the wide area network. Using this scheme, the client would initially contact the server to inquire about the identity of the site that it ought to select to communicate with. The server maintains information that determines the optimum surrogate site for each client. Upon knowing the identity of the client, the server can then direct the client to the right server. Such a redirection protocol can be designed to operate at any layer above the transport layer. Two such tentative protocols are described in the section on the more specific case of client routing in the context of web servers.

3.2.5 Anycast

An alternative method for selecting one out of many servers is to support this notion explicitly as part of the network routing protocols. In the classic anycast scheme, a set of addresses are recognized by the network as being a special type of group communication. This block of addresses is an anycast address. Multiple servers may share an anycast address. The network routing protocols ensure that any packets sent by a client to the anycast address will be received by exactly one of the servers that shares the anycast address.

The anycast protocol may be implemented in a variety of fashions. A simple way to implement the anycast protocol is to broadcast a message to all the servers in the group. Each server responds to the message with its own network address, and the network stack at the client selects the server whose response is the first one to be received back. The client remembers the identity of the server whose response is accepted on the first packet to be sent on the anycast address, and uses it for future communication.

An alternative way to support anycast would be for each router to maintain a link to the nearest server in the anycast group. As servers advertise their membership in the anycast groups to the network, the network routers update the routing tables so that packets can be directed to the nearest server. In this scheme, the routing tables may cause packets to be directed to a different host as new members leave and join. If the client needs to stick with the same server for the duration of a communication, communication with only a single server is required, and the client needs to remember the identity of the server selected on the first packet.

The fundamental limitation of anycast schemes is that they require support from the underlying network. If you do not own the network on which you want to deploy a content distribution solution, it would be difficult to implement this approach. Even if you own the network, you have to ensure that the switches/routers in the infrastructure support the anycast feature. If they do not, upgrading all the devices to a level that supports the anycast feature could be a daunting task.

3.2.6   Wide Area Routing

One approach that can provide effects similar to anycast routing without requiring support for anycast within the network is to exploit the routing infrastructure within a network. The routing protocols within a network are designed to select the shortest path between two points in the network. In the context of a connection-oriented network, the process of routing is invoked when a connection is being established. In the context of a connectionless or datagram network, a background routing process on each device creates a routing table that is then used during the datagram forwarding process.

Most routing schemes divide the problem into two levels: that of determining the shortest route between two points within (loosely speaking) a single administrative domain, and that of determining the shortest route between points within two different administrative domains. Within a single domain, each device maintains either a full topology of the devices within the domain, or maintains a simplified routing table containing the best outgoing link to each of the devices within the domain. Across domains, the routing information is aggregated in order to provide a more scalable solution. The details of the aggregation process depend on the specific protocol being used.

Most routing protocols assume that a destination may be connected to multiple devices within the network. This fact can be exploited to hide the fact that there are multiple sites involved within the network. The operator of the content distribution network publishes its connectivity to the network as if it is a virtual site connected to many different points within the network. Figure 3.4 shows how this concept works. A content distribution network with four sites is shown in the left half of the figure. The right half shows how the connectivity of the site should be advertised by the owner of the content distribution network in order to set the routing tables to go to the nearest site.

Although the use of the routing trick can be made to work with existing network infrastructure, there are a few caveats that must be kept in mind. Many routing schemes aggregate addresses into larger units in order to reduce the size of the routing tables being exchanged. The addresses used for the site must not be aggregated by the network during the process of computing network addresses. This requires that the provider of the content distribution network work closely with the provider of basic networking services. If a very large network comprising several administrative domains is involved, the administrative

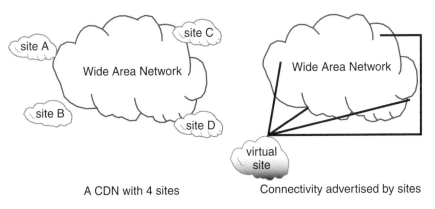

A CDN with 4 sites   Connectivity advertised by sites

Figure 3.4.

issues involved with this scheme can become more complex than the technical issues.

3.2.7 The Final Word

Most of the techniques described above can be used to direct clients to one of the many sites that make up a content distribution network. Depending on the environment one is operating under, one can combine two or more of these techniques to come up with a good working solution. As an example, the client redirection protocol can be used in conjunction with a special directory server. The bulk of selection is done by the directory server mechanism, but in case it happens to end up with the wrong site, the client redirection protocol would ensure that the correct site is selected.

Some of the different mechanisms for a combined approach can be seen in the different solutions that can be used to locate web servers in a wide area environment.

3.3 WIDE AREA LOAD BALANCING MECHANISMS FOR WEB SERVERS

Having looked at the wide area load balancing mechanisms in general, let us take a look at the specific case of web servers and how wide area load balancing can be achieved for this purpose. We will examine the general schemes and see how they can be realized in the context of the HTTP protocol running over TCP/IP networks. Many of the schemes can also be used for client–server interactions based on other protocols running on a TCP/IP network as well.

For the web server illustration, we will take the same example company that we discussed in the previous chapter. The website for the company is available at the URL http://www.company.com. We will also assume that this company uses three sites for its content distribution network. We will refer to these sites as sites A, B, and C. Each of the sites can consist of multiple machines, and the company is using some mechanism to load balance between these sites. Each of the sites needs a valid set of IP addresses over the Internet. We assume that the company has access to three sets of class C addresses—200.0.0.0, 201.0.0.0, and 202.0.0.0. In other words, it can legitimately use any block of address in the range of 200.0.0.0–200.0.0.255, 201.0.0.0–201.0.0.255, and

202.0.0.0–202.0.0.255 on the Internet. The most natural way to use these block of addresses would be to use the 200 addresses for the first site, the 201 addresses for the second site, and the 202 addresses for the third site.

3.3.1 Extensions to Single-Site Load Balancer

The first solution that we can use is that of a front-end load balancer located at one of the sites that is designated as the primary site. Let us assume that site A with a load balancer address of 200.0.0.1 is selected as the primary site. The machine name of the company URL, www.company.com, is advertised to map to the address of 200.0.0.1 in the Internet domain name system. Each client then contacts the load balancer at the first site in order to access a web page belonging to the company. The load balancer decides whether to relay the request onward to one of the servers within its local site, or to relay it toward one of the other sites. This decision may be made depending on the load on the site. Under relatively low loads, the load balancer may decide to serve packets from the local site. When the load increases above a certain threshold, it may decide to route requests to one of the other sites. This solution is an effective way to gain scalability when higher loads are expected at the server, but may not improve user response time due to congestion in the network.

In the simplest mode of operation, the load balancer may act as a reverse surrogate server. It intercepts all communications from the clients and relays them to the appropriate server. The resulting responses are also relayed back to the client. The packets that travel on the wide area network from the load balancer to the other site are similar in structure to the packets that the client sends to the load balancer (except that the load balancer is now acting as the client). There are three front-end load balancers at each site, with the IP addresses 200.0.0.2, 201.0.0.2, and 202.0.0.2. There is a surrogate server operating at 200.0.0.1 that sends a request to one of the three load balancers 200.0.0.2, 201.0.0.2, and 202.0.0.2. The surrogate server operating at 200.0.0.1 sends requests to one of the load balancers and relays back its response to the client. One can also merge the functions of load balancer 200.0.0.2 and surrogate server 200.0.0.1 in a single box, but we will leave them separate in this example.

Surrogate server 200.0.0.1 is acting as a super load balancer located in a tier in front of the three other load balancers of the geographically distributed sites. It needs to perform thrice as fast as the load balancer in front of the different sites. In the previous chapter, we saw that one way for the load balancer to perform better is to avoid acting as a surrogate, operating instead at the level of single IP packets. The techniques enabling this are the use of network address translation and the use of MAC layer addresses with a shared IP address. Let us examine the operation of these techniques in the wide area environment.

The best way to understand these differences is to examine the structure of packets on the wire as it would appear with the use of a surrogate server, using the NAT scheme and using MAC layer addresses with a shared IP address. Let us consider a client with an IP address of 9.0.0.1. This client would send requests to the surrogate server at the well-known address of 200.0.0.1, which would then forward these requests to the load balancer at 201.0.0.2. The load balancer would then forward the packets to a local server, let us say 201.0.0.3. The flows that need to be happen among the different surrogate boxes are shown in Figure 3.5. The source and destination addresses as they would appear on each leg of the flows is also shown in the figure. In this solution, there are at least two different TCP connections established between

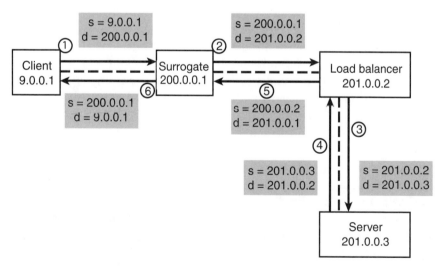

Figure 3.5.

the client and the surrogate server, and between the surrogate server and the load balancer at the remote site. Depending on the nature of the load balancer 201.0.0.2, there may be a third connection between the load balancer and the final server. The TCP connections are as shown by dashed lines in Figure 3.5, which assumes that the load balancers are also acting as surrogate servers.

The surrogate server, as well as the load balancer, can exploit network address translation to produce a more efficient implementation of this scheme. When a NAT solution would be used by the surrogate server, there would be only one TCP connection that would be established between the client and the final server 201.0.0.3. The packets on this connection would be translated as shown in Figure 3.6. The surrogate server at the front-end site simply changes the destination field of the packet to that of load balancer 201.0.0.2 and sends it on the wide area network. The load balancer receives the packet and then translates the destination field to be that of the actual server. The response packets are generated by the server with the source being its IP address of 201.0.0.3, and the load balancer on the surrogate site can translate it back to the globally well-known address of

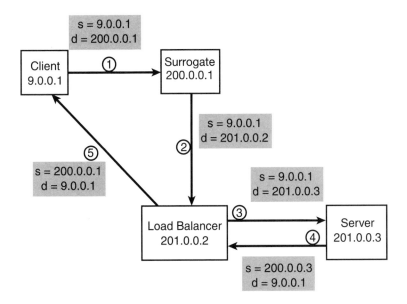

Figure 3.6.

201.0.0.1. In this case, the packets can then travel back from the load balancer to the client directly. They need not go back through the original surrogate server. This is an instance of triangular routing, which can reduce the latency perceived by the client.

Depending on the mode of operation of the load balancer, the reverse translation step may be avoided. If the load balancer is capable of transferring packets to the destination servers on the basis of MAC addresses, then all the servers at the surrogate site can use the common IP address of 200.0.0.1 and there would be no need to have any translation on the reverse path. This will also result in a triangular route.

3.3.2   Triangular Routing Using Mobile IP

We have already seen two examples of triangular routes using front-end load balancers that forward packets at the network level. As it turns out, there is an alternative way to implement triangular routing in IP networks. This technique is based on the use of mobile IP.

The IP protocol was designed to work for devices that stayed in one place rather than move around the network. Once a machine had an IP address, it would stay in the same place. All IP routing protocols are designed with a simple principle in mind: a subnet of IP addresses does not move.

With the emergence of devices that move, e.g., laptop computers, these protocols have become inadequate. Luckily, most laptop computers tend to be clients rather than servers. One other characteristic of the way most laptop computers move is that they are shut down when moving from one site and rebooted when they go to another site. This means that the IP address did not change during the lifetime of a TCP connection. The use of DHCP (Dynamic Host Configuration Protocol) [82] solved many of the problems associated with such clients. The idea behind DHCP is that a subnet of IP addresses would be in a static location with respect to other subnets within the global IP network. As a new machine comes into the subnet, it will ask for and get an address from this pool. This address is granted by a DHCP server which can also provide other network configuration information to the client. It can enable communication with any of the other machines on the global IP network. When the machine is moved to a new location, one can repeat the process of obtaining a new IP address (with or without rebooting the machine).

This still does not solve the problem of some machines that need to move while maintaining an active TCP connection. In order to address those concerns, the mobile IP standard [83] was developed. In the case of mobile IP, each mobile machine had two types of IP addresses: (1) a home address that was fixed and did not change, and (2) a roaming address that was assigned dynamically depending on the location where the machine would be. The machine would always register its roaming address with an agent at the home address, so that packets sent to the home address could be forwarded to the node at its roaming address. The machine could respond back to anyone communicating with it.

So far, the communication will take the path in the standard triangular route situation, but the developers of the mobile IP protocol wanted to find a better solution. Therefore, ongoing work in mobile IP allows a mobile node to inform a communicating peer that its roaming address has actually changed. The peer node's IP stack would take note of this change and use the roaming address instead of the home address for future packets going to the mobile node. Thus, once the change address notification has been implemented, the direct short route instead of the triangular route can be used for communication.

The same mechanism can be exploited by servers in a content distribution network, provided the clients communicating with them have support for mobile IP. The establishment of a communication session between a client and a server would occur in the following steps:

1. A client would send its packets to a well-known address for the server.
2. A load balancer at the well-known location would send the packets to a remote site.
3. A server at the remote site would respond to the message using the original well-known location. It would also notify the client that the address has changed to its actual IP address.
4. When the client received the change address notification, it would use the new address of the selected server. This would then send packets directly to the appropriate server instead of going through the well-known location.

The nice thing about this solution is that the communication follows the direct path between the client and the selected site, and can avoid any congestion that may be present on the path between the client and the home site. However, it requires that the clients support mobile IP, a condition which is currently far from being ubiquitously satisfied.

The change address notification can be seen as an instance of a client redirection protocol that works in conjunction with triangular routing as a default.

3.3.3   Special Directory Servers

The directory system in the case of the TCP/IP protocol suite is the domain name system, and the use of domain name system in this case means giving out the address of the appropriate surrogate site when a client tries to resolve its name. When the query trying to resolve an address comes to a special DNS server, the server will choose the right site and give the address of the load balancer located at that site as the correct answer.

Let us apply this to the case of the three sites that operate for the machine www.company.com in the example we are considering. We need to run a special DNS server. However, there is no need for a special surrogate server (which was 200.0.0.1 in the previous example), but a load balancer is needed at each of the sites in the system. The load balancers for the three sites are 200.0.0.2, 201.0.0.2, and 202.0.0.2, respectively. The DNS server needs to be provide the right address depending on where the client is located.

In order to implement this solution, we need to have control over a DNS server that is considered the primary authority for the names we use for machines at the sites. Primary authority is granted over a DNS domain, rather than on a machine name basis. Therefore, in order to support the example we have listed here, we need to control the domain name server for the domain company.com. If this turns out to be too much control, then we will need to create a subdomain that we can control with our special DNS server. Let us say the domain was web.company.com, and we can adverstise our well-known machine name to be www.web.company.com. The controllers of the full domain company.com simply have to be cooperative enough to configure their domain name server to state that the canonical name for the machine www.company.com happens to be www.web.company.com. This will ensure that the domain name server asks any client name servers querying for www.company.com to query for the name www.web.company.com as well as tells the client name server that our special domain name sever is the authoritative server for the domain web.company.com.

When our special server gets the DNS query request, it examines who has made the right query. Unfortunately, the query does not carry the identity of the client as a field, but our special server can look at the source address of the resolver that made the request. On the basis of this resolver, we select one of the three sites and return that as the the IP address of the machine www.company.com. The client can then connect to the appropriate site.

Let us consider the case of a client that contacts its local domain name server for the name of the machine. If the local domain name server then contacts our special DNS server for the machine name, we can determine the approximate location of the client, and send it to the appropriately selected site (site A). As long as the client's names are being resolved by a DNS server that is reasonably close to them, we can be assured that we are picking a site close to the client.

Unfortunately, the DNS queries are not always guaranteed to come through a name server that is close to the client. When a name server gets to resolve a query for the first time, it does not know which name server to contact. In that case, it forwards the request to the domain name server that serves its parent domain. The process is repeated until it hits a domain name server that has seen the query previously and knows that it should contact our special server, or else it goes to the root domain name server and then comes down to us from our parent domain server. In this case, we really have no idea where the query is originating from, and effectively have to make a random selection.

This situation is shown in Figure 3.7, where the query originates from a location, say ws1.cs.poly.edu, and is looking for the machine www.company.com. The query will first go to the name server for domain cs.poly.edu, then to name server for poly.edu, and then to the name server of .edu. This will be propagated up to the root name server, which will relay it down to the name server of .com, which will then relay it down to our special name server. We really have no idea where the client has come from. However, this is only a transitory situation. When we send back the queries,

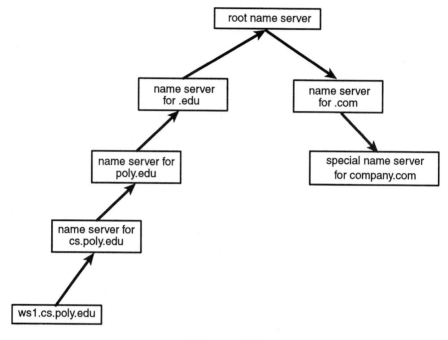

Figure 3.7.

all the name servers along the path will know that our special domain name server is the one to be referred to for the next query to
the name web.company.com.

Another situation that can throw us off balance is the use of a
single name server by a large ISP or organization. Such a large
organization may have many DNS servers throughout the world.
However, it may have configured the domain name servers to
come out only through a single root domain name server that is
located on the west coast of the United States. Even the queries
from the clients in this organization that are located on the east
coast of United States would appear to come from the west coast
of the United States, and our special DNS server would direct
them to the wrong place.

The fact that DNS name servers are not always located at the
same place as the machine originating the query is the weakness
in the use of the DNS server for wide area load balancing. Readers interested in more details on the effectiveness of DNS-based
schemes are referred to [75]. Despite its weakness, this scheme is
the one that can permit wide area load distribution on top of the

existing TCP/IP protocol suite without requiring a change in the underlying infrastructure.

3.3.4 Client Redirection Protocols

A client redirection protocol is a way for a server to tell the client that it should be talking to another server at one of the surrogate sites instead. Such a redirection protocol can be used efficiently to direct a client to the closest server in an efficient manner. The basic operation of any client redirection protocol consists of the following steps:

1. The client sends a message to a server.
2. The server sends a redirection message to the client asking it to contact another server.
3. The client contacts the other server.

Such a client redirection protocol can be developed at any of the different levels in the networking stack. We have already seen an example of such a client redirection protocol in the context of mobile IP. A similar scheme for client redirection exists in the HTTP protocol. A web server can respond to a client server with a redirection request, which can be done by specifying a response code between 300 and 399 in the HTTP protocol. (Only codes 301 through 307 are actually defined in HTTP 1.1 specifications.) The different values of the codes indicate whether the response should be sent to another site permanently or temperarily. A response code of 305 directs a request to a surrogate, a response code of 302 directs a request to another URL for this request only, and a response code of 301 directs the client to use the other site for all future accesses to the specified URL. Any one of these response codes can be used by the server at an origin site to send a client to a surrogate site.

One advantage of the client redirection protocol is that it can take into account the exact location of the client and decide on the most appropriate site to redirect the client to. The main issue with the HTTP redirection is that it is not transparent to the client, and the clients can see that they have been directed to a surrogate site rather than the main site. As a result of this, some clients may choose to bookmark the new surrogate site to visit later. If the surrogate site will always be able to serve the right content, the bookmark may not be an issue. However, if the surrogate servers are only used to offload excess traffic occasionally, the bookmark of the client would fail to work.

An indirect way to build a redirection protocol is to change the content of a web page. In general, most people access the main page of a site and then follow embedded links from the index page. An indirect method of building a redirection protocol is to change the embedded links to point to a surrogate site. The embedded links are then obtained from the surrogate site. This scheme works quite well for loading large objects, e.g., images from a site that is closest to the client.

The main challenge in indirect redirection by rewriting pages is that the pages need to be customized for each client request. If links are embedded in a complex manner in the index page, the customization can increase the amount of time required to serve a page significantly. One alternative would be to use page rewriting in conjunction with some other routing scheme, e.g., replacing links with a special host name whose mapping to a surrogate site can be determined by a modified DNS server. This will enable the same page to be served to all the clients while enabling each client to load embedded links from a close surrogate site (or the site that is selected subject to the limitations of the DNS approach). At the time of writing of this book, this approach was used by the predominant content distribution service provider, Akamai, to deliver images for its customers.

If the number of surrogate sites to which a client can be directed is limited, one can use an approach that precreates several versions of the index page, each with the embedded links pointing to one of the many surrogate sites. When a client request is received, the closest surrogate site to the client is determined, and the corresponding page served to the client.

Since a client redirection protocol exists at the HTTP layer and one exists at the IP layer (as part of mobile IP), it is reasonable to ask whether such a protocol can also exist at the TCP layer. Unfortunately, no such scheme existed for TCP at the time of writing this book. However, it is possible to build such a redirection protocol for TCP by including a special TCP option that requests a client to go to a surrogate site. This TCP option would be included by a server in the response to a connection establishment request, and clients that understand the protocol can go to a closer surrogate site. If you are in a position where you can control the network stack of the clients as well as the servers comprising the content distribution network, such an enhancement to TCP will enable client redirection for any connection-based application on the Internet.

3.3.5 IP Anycast

IP anycast refers to a special mode of routing whereby a request is directed to one of the many servers that are listening on the same address. The anycast mode of routing is supported in IP Version 6, which is the successor to the currently ubiquitous IP Version 4. IP Version 4 does not support anycast routing in the native mode.

If you are running a web server on an IPV6 network, you can obtain content distribution simply by deciding to use a common anycast address for each of the surrogate and origin sites. The IPV6 anycast routing mechanisms would ensure that the clients are directed to exactly one of the servers. The server selected would typically be the one that is closest to the client, with closeness defined by the routing protocol deployed in the network.

In the current IPV4 networks, anycast is not supported. If you are running a web server that would be accessed by a standard web browser, there is no easy way to obtain the effects of an anycast route within the network. If you are running a client program that could be modified, it is possible to build analogues of network layer IP anycast at the application level.

One way to build the application level anycast scheme is to have a special directory service that can determine the right server for any client. Prior to actual communication, the client would consult the directory service to determine the appropriate server. A modified client program in these cases would contact a directory server that would tell it the location of the right server to contact. The directory server needs to maintain a mapping that describes the right server for each of the clients within the network.

An alternative approach would be to form an IP multicast group consisting of all of the servers. The initial request is sent to all of the servers participating in the group. One or more servers may respond, and the client selects the first response as the server to which it ought to communicate. The client then opens a normal TCP connection to the selected server and obtains the data/file it is looking for.

The other approach to mimic anycast in the existing Internet is to trick the routing system to route packets to the site closest to a client as defined by the network routing metric. The approaches that can obtain this result are described in the next section.

3.3.6 Wide Area Routing

Routing within the IP network is generally divided into two categories—routing within a single administrative domain and routing across multiple administrative domains. These are also known as the interior gateway protocols and the exterior gateway protocols. A gateway is the same thing as a router.

The interior gateway protocols can be divided into two categories—the distance vector protocols and the link state protocols. The difference between the two is the manner is which distance information is exchanged among the different routers. Typically, the distance is maintained on the granularity of IP subnets. In a distance vector protocol, each node maintains a table showing its distance from a given subnet. The nodes exchange their copy of the table among themselves. On each message received from a peer, the node checks to see if there is a shorter path available to any of the destination subnets, and if so the table is updated and the resulting table propagated to other peers of the node. After a few exchanges, each node has the shortest path to the listed destination subnets. In a link state protocol, each node maintains the full topology of the network. The status of a link (whether it is up or down) is propagated to the nodes in the network, which will update their graphs accordingly. The graphs are then used to compute the shortest distance to any destination.

If your CDN solution is going to operate in an enterprise environment where you have an interior gateway protocol running, you can exploit the routing schemes to direct clients to the closest server. The operator of the network needs to agree to maintain the subnet running your CDN sites as a separate entry in its routing tables. If so, you simply advertise the connectivity information of your different CDN sites to the routers most closely attached to your sites within the network. The routers will propagate the connectivity information, and each client will be directed to the nearest site.

The nice feature of the routing scheme is that it leverages the underlying protocols of the network layer in a very efficient manner, and does not require any distance accounting on the part of the CDN. It also brings a client to the closest (in terms of network hops) site. However, network routing protocols do not take into account the load on a server, so this scheme will not be able to result in spreading the load evenly across different sites. Another drawback of the scheme is that it needs the cooperation of the network operator, which limits the environments under which it can be applied.

If you need to have the CDN sites connected to the Internet, you will need to use a similar scheme to work with the exterior gateway protocols. The exterior gateway protocols were defined to operate across multiple administrative domains and multiple network operators. At this level, most network operators like to merge the number of destination IP addresses in order to reduce the size of their routing tables. Since it is unlikely that you can persuade all of the network operators in the Internet to leave the subnet corresponding to your scheme alone, the scheme may not be as effective as in the case when dealing with a single network provider. However, you can achieve much of the same result by connecting to more than one network operator at each of the CDN sites. Most network operators prefer to carry as much of the traffic as they can themselves, sending packets to another operator only when there is no other choice. Therefore, if your CDN sites are connected to multiple ISPs at each of the sites, there will be multiple paths advertised within the network for your site, and the clients will be distributed among the many sites.

Given the coarse granularity at which IP routing protocols operate, these routing tricks are useful when you have a small number of sites and each site is located in a different geographic location. Thus, a large company may use this technique to direct users to one of its four portals, e.g., in Europe, Asia, South America, or the United States, depending on where the client originates.

3.4 CONCLUSION

In this chapter, we have looked at mechanisms that can be used to direct clients to the right server. This is one half of the problem. We will take a look at the other half—how to determine which site is the closest one for the user—in the next chapter.

4 Selecting the Right Site in a CDN

A CDN consists of many sites and when a client request is received, the request needs to be directed to the site that is the best matched to the client. In this chapter, we look at the different techniques that can be used to determine the appropriate server site.

The definition of the best site is one that deserves some discussion. It depends on the purpose for which the CDN is designed. A CDN may be deployed in order to minimize the response time to a client. In that case, the best site would be defined by its proximity to the client and by the amount of traffic experienced at each of the sites. In other cases, the CDN is developed to improve the scalability of the server site, with the client response only being secondary. In this case, the best site would be the one that has the least current load at a given time.

The schemes that can be used to select the right site for a client include active probing, the use of a static routing map, and the use of a dynamic routing map. In the next few sections, we look at each of these techniques in more detail. As in the previous chapters, we start with a discussion of the general techniques, and then provide detailed explanations of how each scheme would work in the Internet.

4.1 GENERAL SCHEMES FOR SITE DETERMINATION

The schemes for determining a site can be divided into two categories: (1) active monitoring when a request is received, and (2) passive schemes using routing tables. An active scheme is a scheme that requires the generation of extra packets within the network when a request is received. A passive scheme does not require the generation of extra packets on the arrival of the request. Instead, a table mapping different clients and requests to the best

85

suitable site is created and used to direct clients appropriately. The operation and maintenance of the routing table requires the flow of extra packets in the network, but these are not coupled to a specific request.

4.1.1   Active Schemes with Per-Request Monitoring

An active scheme is a scheme that requires the generation of extra packets within the network. The extra packets are generated to measure the network characteristics and server load at the various sites within the network. Such generation triggered at the instance of the arrival of a client request at a decision maker. As an example, if a directory-server-based technique is used for wide area load balancing, the special directory server would initiate the active mechanism when it receives a query request from a new source. The directory server is the decision maker in this case. In other cases, the decision maker may be a surrogate server or a front-end load balancer.

The type of extra packets generated by this mechanism depends on the goal of the content distribution network. If the goal of the content distribution network is to improve the scalability of the servers, i.e., handle most requests possible, the request should be routed to the server that is the least loaded one. An active scheme would determine the least loaded server by having the decision maker send a probe message to each of the sites. A performance monitoring server at each of the sites would respond to the probe message by including an estimate of the current load at the site. The decision maker could then select the server with the least load.

When the goal of a content distribution network is to reduce the response time of a user, we need to select a site that would be closest to the user. In this case, the performance monitoring server would monitor the distance of the client from its site, and return a metric for the client distance to the decision maker. The decision maker would then select the site with the smallest distance and then inform the client of the selection.

When the performance monitor at the site gets a probe message, it can measure the distance to the client or its load explicitly. Alternatively, it may have learned the distances to the client from past experience, and may be monitoring the load on its site at periodic intervals. In these cases, the performance monitor may send the most recent such measurement to the decision maker.

4.1.2 Passive Schemes Using a Routing Table

When a passive scheme using a routing table is used, the decision maker maintains a routing table that can map the incoming requests to the best site for the request. Such a routing table would typically have two fields—the first field identifying a group of clients, and the second field identifying one of the CDN sites. When a request arrives at the decision maker, the decision maker would consult the routing table to determine the best sites for the client, and return the location of that site to the user.

In some cases, the routing decision may not only be based on the location of the client, but also on the resource a client may wish to access. In these cases, one can also build a routing table that maps a client trying to access a specific resource to one of the many sites within a CDN. In this case, the routing table will have three fields—the first one identifying the client, the second one identifying the resource, and the third one identifying the closest site. For each incoming request, the client's location and the resource being requested are identified and used to look up the appropriate site from the routing table.

The routing table itself is made up from a routing information matrix that provides a distance metric between each client and the site (or in the case of a resource-specific entry, provides a distance metric for a client accessing a resource at a site). The distance metric could be the round trip latency from the client to the site, the load on the specific site, or a combination of the two. Let us consider a global CDN with three sites located in New York, Paris, and New Delhi. Clients for this CDN may originate in Europe, the Americas, Asia, or Africa. Let us consider the simpler case in which routing is based solely on the location of the client. The routing information matrix for this CDN may look like that shown in Table 4.1, where the distance metric reflects the average round trip latency between a user and the appropriate site. On the basis of this routing information matrix, the decision maker will create a routing table that looks like Table 4.2, and will route users in the Americas to New York, users in Europe and Africa to Paris, and the users in Asia to New Delhi.

When some of the resources are available at some sites and not

Table 4.1   Sample routing information matrix

Client location	Surrogate server	Distance metric
Europe	New York	120
The Americas	New York	30
Asia	New York	160
Africa	New York	160
Europe	Paris	30
The Americas	Paris	120
Asia	Paris	160
Africa	Paris	100
Europe	New Delhi	160
The Americas	New Delhi	200
Asia	New Delhi	60
Africa	New Delhi	120

at others, the distance metric in the routing information matrix may be different for each type of resource. As an example, a streaming video server may only be available in New York and Paris, but not in New Delhi. In this case, the routing information matrix would have an additional column showing the resource type, and the distance metric would incorporate the availability or the performance of the resource available at that site.

The routing information matrix may be created in a static manner, and the corresponding routing table determined statically for the entire system. However, this is not likely to be as effective as the case when the routing information matrix is maintained in a dynamic manner to reflect the most recent network and server state.

Dynamic routing matrix information can be maintained by all the sites monitoring the performance characteristics of clients that access them. The performance monitoring can be based on passive observation of a client's traffic, or it may be done by active

Table 4.2   Sample routing table

Client location	Surrogate server
The Americas	New York
Europe	Paris
Africa	Paris
Asia	New Delhi

means, e.g., by sending a probe packet to the client, or having the client generate a probe message of some type. The different sites can then report their collective performance statistics to the decision maker, who can combine the different reports together into a routing information matrix, and then generate a routing table.

Instead of a centralized approach that relies on a single decision maker to merge the performance information collected by the sites into the routing information matrix, a distributed approach can also be used to make the routing information matrix/routing table. The distributed routing approach would have the different sites exchanging their performance information with each other, each site forming a composite routing table from the information thus received. The decision maker can obtain the routing table (or the routing information matrix) from its local site. The distributed approach enables any of the sites to act as a decision maker.

The passive routing table scheme works well if one can obtain good performance characteristics related to a client's access to a site. If a client (or another client in the same general vicinity) has visited the CDN before, it is likely to show up in the routing table thus formed. However, on the first ever visit of a client to the decision maker, no proximity information for the client may be available. A combination of the active and the passive schemes can be used in this case. If information about a client can be found in the routing table, it is used to route the client. If no information is found, an active approach is used instead, or a default site is selected.

In the rest of the chapter, we examine how these approaches can be used for routing web browser requests on a CDN deployed within the Internet.

4.2 ACTIVE SCHEMES FOR CLIENT ROUTING ON WEB CDNs

In a web-based CDN, active schemes involve having one of the many potential web sites determine actively the distance between themselves and a client. The most common way in which this distance is measured is by using the ICMP echo or the ping mechanism.

ICMP [25] is a control protocol supported by all devices that implement the IP protocol. One of its options allows one IP machine to send an ICMP echo request to another IP machine. In response to the echo request, the second IP machine sends back an echo reply. By measuring the time between the transmission of the request and the receipt of the response, the first machine can determine the network delay with the second machine. The process of sending the request and measuring the response is called pinging, because the application program that performs this operation is named "ping" on most operating systems.

An active mechanism for the web pages can then be constructed as follows. The decision maker for a web server CDN could be either a specialized DNS server or a surrogate server/load balancer. When the decision maker receives a request, it sends a probe message to all of the web servers involved in the CDN. Each web server pings the client machine to get the network delay from the client. The response to the probe message can also include a measure of how much load the server is currently experiencing, e.g., a count of currently active sessions. The decision maker can choose the site with the least delay to the client, the least load, or an appropriate weight between the two.

The advantage of pinging the clients on a per-request basis is that one can determine exactly which site is closest to the client under the current state of the network. However, if the number of CDN sites is large, such ping messages can generate significant traffic on the network. Furthermore, the steps of sending the probe messages, pinging the clients, and collecting the responses, add a significant amount of delay to the time it takes a client to receive a response from the decision maker. If the page being accessed by the client is short, the overhead of determining the right server can easily outweigh the gains of selecting a closer site.

One way to alleviate these problems is to cache the results of prior measurements. When the decision maker is a reverse surrogate, it is likely that the same client is going to make many requests to the server. In this case, the overhead of selecting the right site is paid only on the first request. When the decision maker is a DNS server, the queries come indirectly through the name server of the client. Since name servers will normally cache the results of the response and repeat a request only when the cached entry expires, the caching of the measurements at the decision maker may be less effective.

When the decision maker is a reverse surrogate, it can exploit the active code technology supported by most common browsers to have the client actively measure and select the right site for a web page. The scheme involves sending a page containing a portion of active code to the client, e.g., a Java applet or a Javascript program. The applet/script would then invoke a monitoring URL at all of the websites. The monitoring URL would provide a simple response, and the applet/script could measure the time taken for the response to come back. The applet/script would then select the site with the best response characteristics and load the full contents of the page from the appropriate site and display it in the browser's window.

This scheme would be useful when the pages being downloaded are large (e.g., contain many large graphic images). However, the support of applets and Javascript program across web browsers varies tremendously across different browsers, and even among different versions of the same browser. Making a piece of active code work across all browsers is tricky. The security settings of some browsers may not permit the active code to access the remote URL, or the settings of some browsers may not permit a redirection of the main browser window. Therefore, such an approach is likely to work only in environments where the browser version can be controlled. If your CDN is supported within an enterprise, and you can issue an enterprise-wide directive that only one specific version of a browser be used, this approach can be used. On the open Internet, using an active code approach can open a Pandora's box of trying to track different browser's capabilities.

4.3   USING A ROUTING TABLE IN WEB-BASED CDNs

A more efficient manner to route client requests to the appropriate server would be to maintain a routing table that maps the users to the right server. In the context of the Internet, clients are identified by their IP addresses. Routing [26] is usually done on the basis of a group of IP addresses that define a subnetwork (subnet). The common usage of network routing has tended to define subnets so that all machines in the same subnet have a common prefix. The reader would recall that Internet addresses are 32 bits long, and typically written by taking the decimal value of each byte (8 bits) with a dot separating them. The subnet is commonly expressed as the address of the first machine on the subnet and the length of the common shared prefix. Thus, the subnet 9.2.20.0/24 defines all IP addresses whose first 24 bits are the same as that in the address 9.2.20.0.

A routing table for the decision maker would therefore consist of entries mapping subnets to the site most appropriate for clients coming from that subnet. The site may be identified by any unique identifier. If each of the sites has a different IP address, the IP address may be used as an identifier; if they have different domain names, the domain name can be used. If the different sites have the same IP addresses and domain names, the identifier could be the MAC address of the load balancer at each of the sites.

The routing table can be constructed in a variety of ways. The construction of the routing table and the routing information matrix may be done statically and modified only rarely, or it can be created and updated dynamically. The static routing table would need to be constructed on the basis of the Internet topology that is available for a network route. The dynamic routing table requires that each site collect performance statistics about the clients accessing it. The performance statistics can then be combined together in various ways to construct a routing table.

4.3.1   Static Routing Table

A static routing table can be constructed if the topology of the network that clients would use to communicate with the sites in the CDN is known. If the connectivity of the clients to the different sites is known, one can determine a priori which sites the client ought to be directed to.

The addressing structure within enterprise intranets as well as the Internet tends to follow a hierarchical structure. This hierarchy helps in defining the routing table and keeping it manageable. An enterprise intranet usually consists of several campus sites that are then connected together by the wide area links. Some of the campus sites host the servers that participate in the CDN. The other campus sites are the clients accessing the CDN. It is conventional for all the machines in the same campus to belong to a single IP subnet. Thus, the main task in determining a static routing table is to determine which of the CDN sites is closest to each of the client sites within the network.

Figure 4.1 shows a typical enterprise intranet that is shown with 14 campus sites. Each campus is shown as a cloud with the

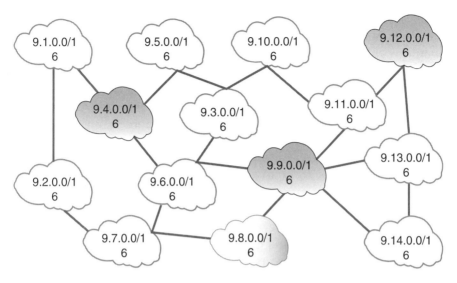

Figure 4.1.

IP subnet assigned to the machines at the campus shown inside the cloud. Three of these sites (shown as shaded clouds in the figure) are parts of the CDN sites where server sites are hosted. Let us assume that the servers that cooperate together in the CDN are 9.4.0.2, 9.9.0.2, and 9.12.0.2.

In order to generate a static routing table or a routing information matrix, one needs to run some simple algorithms on the connectivity graph shown in Figure 4.1. The goal is to determine the site in the CDN that is closest to each of the campuses. The closeness can be determined by assigning a cost to each of the links in the graph; the closest site to a campus is the site that has the lowest-cost path to the campus. The cost of each link can be defined in may ways, e.g., it can be a constant, proportional to the delay on the link, or be a function of the link capacity and delay. A constant cost function will minimize the number of links a client traverses to the selected CDN site. The use of the link propagation delay would minimize the latency between the client and the selected CDN site.

Once such a cost metric has been defined and the graph topology is known, it is relatively straightforward to compute the lowest-cost path in the graph between all the client campuses. This provides the routing information matrix, and the routing table is obtained by simply selecting the most appropriate server for each set of clients within the Intranet. The routing table that would result is shown in Table 4.3.

A static mapping technique can also be used for web servers that operate on the Internet. One concern here is that the subnets that make up the Internet are much more numerous than those within the largest enterprises. The other, more important, concern is that is that Internet connectivity information is not as readily available as an enterprise intranet topology. The topology of the Internet has to be discovered. Note, however, that we are only interested in a subset of the Internet topology. We want to know the distance from each of the CDN sites to the different subnets that make up the Internet.

One way to discover this limited Internet topology is by looking at the BGP (Border Gateway Protocol) tables of the the ISPs that provide connectivity to each of the sites. The BGP routing table contains information about the different subnets known to the ISP routers and the number of different administrative domains (AS hops) that are to be crossed to reach that subnet. This provides the routing information matrix from the vantage point of a single site. If you combine the information from all of the sites, and route each subnet in the BGP tables to the site with the shortest AS hops, you have created a routing table for the clients on the Internet.

Table 4.3 Routing table for example enterprise

Client location	Server	Shortest path length
9.1.0.0/16	9.4.0.2	1
9.2.0.0/16	9.4.0.2	1
9.3.0.0/16	9.4.0.2	2
9.4.0.0/16	9.4.0.2	0
9.5.0.0/16	9.4.0.2	1
9.6.0.0/16	9.4.0.2	1
9.7.0.0/16	9.9.0.2	2
9.8.0.0/16	9.9.0.2	1
9.9.0.0/16	9.9.0.2	0
9.10.0.0/16	9.12.0.2	2
9.11.0.0/16	9.12.0.2	1
9.12.0.0/16	9.12.0.2	0
9.13.0.0/16	9.12.0.2	1
9.14.0.0/16	9.9.0.2	1

The BGP routes only provide access to the best path as determined by the routing tables of the Internet. This should be adequate in many instances, but if you are looking for a metric such as network round-trip latency or number of actual router hops traversed, the BGP routing tables will not be able to provide that information. In this case, one would need to determine the topology information that provides the right performance metrics. One approach is to determine the appropriate subnets that need to be monitored within the Internet, e.g., by looking at the BGP routing table information. Then select some addresses within each subnet and use tools like traceroute and ping to measure the performance of a path from each CDN site to the selected host. The information is then collected to obtain the right performance metric about each of the clients.

Doing any of these measurements over the Internet requires measurements over a period of several days. The information is also subject to change depending on the Internet dynamics. However, the result would be a static map that could be used to efficiently route clients to one of the different CDN sites by means of a simple look-up.

4.3.2 Dynamic Routing Table

The main limitation of a static routing table is that it does not always route a client to the best CDN site. Internet delays, congestion, and routing tables continuously change due to variations in traffic and usage pattern. A site that was selected for routing clients based on information collected at any specific time may not be the best site a year after the information is collected. A dynamic routing table is a routing table that is continuously updated to reflect the best site for any given client.

In order to build a dynamic routing table, one needs to take the following steps:

1. Identify the subnets from which clients are coming.
2. Collect performance statistics between each subnet and each of the CDN sites.
3. Combine the performance statistics at each site to come up with a routing table.

The steps are the same as in the creation of a static routing table, except that the static routing table can be created prior to a

CDN going on line, whereas dynamic routing tables would typically be created and modified with information obtained while a site is on line. Thus, dynamic routing tables can exploit information such as web logs, packet traces, and other information that an on-line site can record.

Each of these steps are described further in the subsections below.

4.3.2.1 Client Clustering

Client clustering refers to the process of identifying the different client subnets that are to be used for building a routing table. The simplest case of client clustering is that of identifying the campus networks within an enterprise. In many enterprises, identifying the subnets of each campus is relatively trivial. If you are designing a CDN for such an enterprise, this step is hardly worth mentioning. However, if you are deploying a CDN for the Internet, the identification of the subnet may be a significant challenge.

One way to define the client clusters is to look at the subnet addresses that are exposed by the BGP routing tables of the ISPs that provide connectivity to the different sites. The set of IP subnets they use to route packets to and from each site provide a good metric for the different clients that will have the same path to each of the sites. The BGP information can identify a subnet and the AS hop to that subnet from a specific site. If the set of subnets thus obtained for one site differs from the set of subnets from other sites, this information can be easily combined. Since each IP address has to be in one of the subnets, the only possibility is that a subnet in the list for the first site has an overlap with a different subnet for the second site. Breaking the common set of addresses into individual client clusters would be adequate in these cases.

If BGP route information is not available, another approach would be to analyze the web logs that are available at the server. Most web servers collect logs on each client access that record information such as the IP address of the accessing client, the URL being accessed, and the bytes transferred as a result. One can start with a division of the entire Internet address space into a group of class C addresses (i.e., subnets with a network prefix 24 bits long). There are 2×24 such subnets, and clearly not all will be active clients at the cluster. One can go through the logs to analyze the top 100 (or 1000) such subnet addresses that account for the most entries in the logs.

As a footnote, the analysis of the log to determine the top 100 sites does not need to keep track of all 10×24 clusters. If the software creates an entry for a client cluster only when needed (e.g., the first time the cluster is seen in the log), the number of entries created would be closer to the top count. One can also take an approach of using no more than $k \times 100$ entries (with k in range 1.25–3) by creating an entry only when needed, and replacing entries that are least recently used and have the lowest frequency of use when no free entry is available.

It would be reasonable to expect that a few clusters will account for most of the accesses to a website. Thus, it would be reasonable to expect that the top 100 or 1000 class C client clusters would account for most of the requests to a site. These are the basic clusters that need to be determined. Clusters that generate less load need not be determined.

Studies of clustering algorithms [27] indicates that use of BGP table information improves the accuracy of clustering when clients need to be clustered according to the routes they will follow to a server. However, if clients need to be clustered in accordance with domain name hierarchies, simple clustering may be reasonably accurate. Some other approaches to clustering clients so as to infer their geographic location can be found in [76].

4.3.2.2   *Collecting Client Performance Metrics*
When a site is operational, each site can record information about the performance that a client experiences when accessing the site. The relative performance of a client when accessing a site is the major factor driving the routing decisions for future requests made to the CDN from that client.

The simplest type of performance monitoring can be done by having a performance monitor at a site. The performance monitor could be implemented as a surrogate server or a web server plug-in. The surrogate server tracks the time that elapses between a request arrival and its response being completed at the site and records that in a log. These logs can then be analyzed and the average response time experienced by clients in a particular cluster determined. A plug-in is a module that performs some function in a web server, except that the function is built as an extension to the web server. Most current web servers offer a modular architecture that enables such a plug-in to be installed statically (at compile time) or dynamically link in new plug-in modules. For the purpose of performance monitoring, a reverse surrogate dedicated to performance monitoring is likely to have more accurate results than a plug-in. This is because different plug-in modules in common web server architectures may be called at different stages of request processing, and it is tricky to ensure that the performance monitoring plug-in is called after all processing on generating a response is completed, and before any processing when a request is received.

Another type of performance monitoring can be done by examining the packets that come with a website. The packets can be collected by means of sniffing machines that are dedicated to the job of collecting packet traces at a site. The packet headers include information such as the beginning of a request, the completion of the response, the beginning and end of connections, as well as the round-trip delay to a client measured by the TCP protocol processing. These packet traces can be analyzed to determine the average delays to a client cluster, or the average response time experienced by clients in a cluster.

An alternative approach to obtain the response time of clients is the use of web bugs. A web bug is an invisible graphic (created in a size too small for a human to see) that loads a blank image from a server. A web bug can be used to measure the average time it would take for a simple operation to be done between the client and the server. As an example, a web bug can be introduced by a site http://www.company.com, invoking an image at the URL http://www.company.com/monitor?image=<timestamp>.gif, where the <timestamp> field is created dynamically to measure the time when the client made the request for the page. When attempting to retrieve the image, a cgi-bin program or a servlet is invoked at the site than computes and records the difference between the time stamp measured as passed in the argument and the current time at the server. This measurement can be used an approximation of the time taken for the request to be sent to the client and the request to be received back at the server.

If the client sites that one needs to monitor can be installed with a performance monitoring tool, it would be possible to monitor the actual performance experienced by a site, rather than the estimates made at the server. If a CDN is being deployed in the context of an enterprise intranet, the clients may have a performance monitoring tool installed on their systems (see [71] for an example of such a tool). In these cases, the performance of the clients can be obtained by examining the results of the performance monitor. As long as the performance monitoring tool is running on at least one client computer at each site, a reasonable estimate of the client performance from that site can be obtained.

In the context of CDNs deployed on the Internet, there are some service providers (Keynote Systems among others [72, 73]) that offer performance monitoring from many servers located throughout the Internet. The performance monitoring data from such service providers at each of the CDN sites can be used as an approximation of actual client performance data. If the client clusters are located near one of the performance monitoring nodes of such a service provider, the data reported by the service provider can be used as an approximation of the actual performance.

As a result of the these monitoring schemes, or a combination of the above, one can determine the relative cost of a client accessing any given site within a CDN. The performance information then needs to be consolidated to form a routing table for the entire CDN. This may be done in a centralized manner or a distributed manner.

4.3.2.3 *Centralized Route Computation*

Centralized route computation is the simplest scheme for combining the performance statistics obtained from each of the different sites participating in a CDN. In this scheme, there is a single routing entity responsible for combining the performance information from each of the sites and consolidating it into a routing table. This routing entity would periodically collect performance statistics from each of the sites, consolidate all the information into a routing information matrix, and then create a single routing table by mapping each client cluster to the site with the best performance.

The collection of performance statistics by the routing entity can be done by having the routing entity poll each of the sites, or the sites can send the updates to the routing entity on their own. The statistics may be collected as raw logs from which the routing entity can collect the information needed for clustering. Alternatively, the clustering of performance statistics can be done by each of the sites and the routing entity can simply do the consolidation of the information.

A centralized routing approach is particularly well suited to environments in which the decision maker (the entity sending the clients to one of the CDN sites) is a centralized one. In this case, the routing entity and the decision maker should be colocated and the decision maker should have access to the latest routing information. A centralized routing entity can also be used with distributed decision makers. Each decision maker then needs to get the updated copy of the routing table whenever it changes. The updated routing table may be fetched periodically by the decision maker, or the routing entity can notify the decision maker whenever a new copy of the routing table is available. If the number of CDN sites is relatively small, a centralized routing entity may be the more efficient and simpler solution.

4.3.2.4 *Distributed Client Routing*

A centralized routing solution can run into scaling problems if the number of sites involved in a CDN are large. In these cases, a distributed scheme for composing the routing tables may be more appropriate. A distributed routing scheme may also be a more natural solution when the decision makers are distributed. If each site has a front-end load balancer that can direct clients to the most appropriate site, the sites can run a distributed routing protocol among themselves to decide which site is best for a client.

In the distributed routing solution, each of the sites would compute the distance between the clients and the local site on the basis of the performance statistics. The sites would then exchange this information with each other. Each site would incorporate the information obtained from other sites to compile an independent routing table themselves.

There are various schemes that can be used to build the routing table in a distributed fashion. One of the simplest schemes would require that all of the sites participate in a single multicast group. Each site broadcasts its performance statistics to the multicast group, and each of the sites would combine the information to form the distributed routing table. In this case, each of the sites is performing the functions of the central routing entity independently. Another way to distribute the routing information would be to create a set of overlay connections among the sites. The routing table could be sent along the overlay links. The overlay approach would be advantageous if multicast was not supported on the wide area network connecting the sites.

When an overlay solution is used, a site may relay the performance statistics from other sites unmodified along the overlay. An alternative option would be that each site consolidate the information received from its neighbors and only forward information about the closest site to each of the links. The reader can readily see that these two schemes are manifestations of the traditional link state routing protocols (e.g., OSPF) and distance vector routing protocols (RIP, EIGRP) used in traditional IP routing. The issues and trade-offs involved in the client routing protocol are virtually identical to those in the better-developed field of IP routing [26].

5 CDN Data Sharing Schemes

Any computer application can be divided into two components: (1) code and (2) data. The code is the program that is executed to invoke the application, whereas data refers to the information that is retrieved or modified by the code. The data may be stored in any persistent form, e.g., as files in the file system of the computer, as records in a database, or as entries in a directory server. Any interaction of a client with the application can result in the retrieval or modification of the data. When applications are run at distributed sites (as in a CDN), each site needs to maintain its own copy of code as well as data. For a consistent operation, each CDN needs to deploy techniques that will enable the sites to share code and data among themselves.

In Chapter 1, we defined the CDN as consisting of one origin site and one or more surrogate sites. The surrogate sites and the origin site can share the same data and code in various ways. The surrogates may access the data at the origin site remotely, replicate all or part of the data at the origin site, and cache all or part of the data at the origin site. Each of these schemes, along with their own merits and demerits, is discussed in Section 5.1.

When data is replicated or cached, the multiple copies of the same information maintained at the different sites can become inconsistent. Thus, consistency schemes that will enable the data at various sites to work together need to be devised for a CDN. The various options for managing consistency are discussed in Section 5.2.

Section 5.3 presents a discussion of the different types of data that make up a typical application and the different ways in which a surrogate server can maintain the relevant types of data. Finally, Section 5.4 shows how to bring all these topics together to construct various data sharing schemes for a web server.

5.1   DATA SHARING SCHEMES

Broadly speaking, the different types of data sharing schemes that can be used by the different surrogates can be divided into three categories: (1) transparent remote access, (2) replicated copies, and (3) caching. In the transparent remote access scheme, a singe copy of data is maintained at the origin site and the surrogate sites access it remotely. In the replicated copies scheme, an independent copy of data is maintained at different sites. Each of these sites act as peers and different schemes can be used to manage the consistency among them. In the caching scheme, the copy of data at the origin site is the official copy, and the surrogate sites maintain a cached copy of a subset of the data.

5.1.2   Transparent Remote Access

In a transparent remote access scheme, there is only one copy of the data. It is maintained at the origin site. The surrogates simply access the data at the origin site. This access to the data in a transparent manner is provided by means of a middleware layer, e.g., a special file system, or a remote procedure call facility. One scheme would be to use the remote mounting facility available in most common file systems, which can enable a file system physically resident at the origin site to be mounted as a network file system by machines at the surrogate site [28]. Another alternative would be for the machines in the surrogate site to make a remote procedure call [29] to access the data available at the remote site. The use of remote procedure invocation can hide the location of a file system or a database from the application. As an example, the remote method invocation [30] scheme of the Java programming language combined with its database access interface JDBC [31] enables an application to access a remote database transparently. Other distributed programming architectures, e.g., CORBA [32], can also be used to enable transparent access to remote data.

The big advantage of the transparent remote access scheme is that it does not require any awareness on the part of the applications that are executing in a CDN. The technologies for remote access, e.g., CORBA, Java-RMI, etc. are well established in the industry. Since a single copy of the data is maintained, the consistency issues are relatively simple.

The remote access paradigm is an ideal solution when the network latency between the users of the data and the copy of the data is low. If multiple machines are connected together with a fast local area network, one of them can export its file system, which others mount over the network. The access latency on the remotely mounted system would be relatively small. Similarly, a machine can host a database and the others may access it using Java RMI. The scheme of having a single copy of data with remote users is a perfectly fine solution as long as the latency between the users and data is relatively low.

When the network latency between the users of the data and the copy of the data is relatively high, transparent remote access does not work very well. Recall that the basic motivation for having a content distribution network is to obtain performance gains by eliminating the client's need to go to the origin server, since the network between the client and origin server is likely to be congested. The link between the surrogate and the origin site is also likely to be congested, since the surrogate and the client are likely to be in the same area of the network. In this case, accessing the data remotely is not likely to reduce the client-perceived response time of the system. When the delay between the surrogate and the origin sites is large, the delays incurred in the remote access to the data can add up significantly.

In some cases, it is possible to have the remote transparent access scheme perform relatively well even in a CDN in which the latency between the different sites is large. If the data access latency in an application is only a minor component of the total processing time, such a scheme will suffice. Consider an application that performs a complex multidimensional graphical display of a database. If the time required for rendering graphics is large relative to the time required to access the data itself, it is quite acceptable to have all the data at a single site and retrieve it when demand for them arises.

In the case of an Internet-based CDN, the CDN sites may be connected together by a private network that could provide a faster access between the sites than similar access over the open Internet. Depending on the characteristics of the private network, maintaining a single copy of the data may be an adequate solution.

5.1.2 Replicated Copies

In the replicated copy paradigm, each CDN site has a full copy of the entire data that may be needed by an application. Each CDN site has equal authority over the data and any application simply needs to access the local copy of the data in order to perform its reads/writes on the data. When a CDN site consists of many individual computers, the access internal to the site may be done by means of a transparent access scheme. Maintaining replicated copies of the data would provide the best performance as far as the latency in performing an operation on the data is concerned.

As mentioned earlier, any request that a user makes to an application can also be divided into two categories: (1) reading and formatting data and (2) modifying or changing the data that is maintained at a site. The formatting refers to changing the format in which data is presented, e.g., database entries may be formatted with HTML tags so as to be suitable for presentation in a browser. If most of the requests were for reading and formatting data, replication can offer substantial gains in performance and scalability. However, when an update request happens, the distributed nature of the data creates two additional concerns: (1) ensuring synchronization between conflicting updates from two different caching surrogates and (2) ensuring consistency of the data cached at the various surrogates, i.e., making sure that a surrogate that has previously cached the piece of data gets the new updated version. In these cases, one has to use a variety of schemes to ensure that the updates are propagated consistently to all of the copies of the data. These consistency schemes are discussed later on in the chapter.

Maintaining fully replicated copies of data requires the maximum storage space across the entire CDN site. However, if the cost of storage space required is within the cost parameters, replication can result in substantial performance gains. The gains are greater for data that is relatively static in nature, i.e., data that is not likely to change very much. Since most of the complexities in managing the consistency of the data arises from operations that modify the data, maintaining replicated copies improves performance as the ratio of read operations to write operations increases. For data that virtually never changes, e.g., an archive of old songs or an archive of photographs, replicated copies provide an ideal solution. A more detailed discussion of replication-based systems in the context of web-servers, databases, and distributed systems can be found in [33], [34], and [35].

5.1.3 Caching

The caching scheme can be looked upon as a mixture of the replicated copies scheme and the transparent remote access scheme. As in the transparent remote access scheme, there is an official copy of data at the origin site, and the surrogate sites depend upon the official copy to obtain data that they may need. As in the replicated copies scheme, some of the data is maintained locally at the surrogate site. However, the data at the surrogate need not be a full replication of all the data at the database. Only a part of the data is replicated at the cache.

When requests arrive for executing operations at the surrogate site, the surrogate would attempt to satisfy the request from the locally cached data. If the data required to satisfy the request is not present at the surrogate, the data is retrieved from the origin site. This data can be stored at the cache for satisfying future requests. The above description is for the pull mode of the cache, in which the cache pulls data from the origin site as needed. There is another way to bring data into the cache using the push mode, in which the data distribution to the cache is initiated by the origin site, i.e., data is pushed to the cache. In the push mode, if a request cannot be satisfied at the cache, it is forwarded to the origin site. Practical caches can use either of the two modes or a mixed mode in which data can be pushed as well as pulled on demand from the origin site.

The performance increase due to caching is based on the principle of locality. The concept of locality originates from virtual memory systems in computers and refers to the phenomenon that computer programs do not access all the pages of their address space uniformly. Since some pages tend to be accessed more frequently than others, keeping those pages in the main memory improves the performance of programs running in virtual memory environments.

The concept of locality is applicable to general caching in wide area networks. As mentioned earlier, any application can be seen as program accessing data items. Applications do not tend to use data in a uniform manner. At any time that an application is executing, the application tends to make repeated access to the same set of data. In other words, many applications exhibit locality of reference. In a qualitative sense, locality measures the clustering of data access that is typical of the behavior of many programs. In the context of the geographically distributed applications, three types of locality can be identified. Temporal locality refers to the fact that at any given time, some pieces of data will be repeatedly accessed by the application. Spatial locality refers to the fact that an application that accesses a piece of data is more likely to access other pieces of related data. Geographical locality refers to the fact that some types of data are more likely to be accessed from one geographical location than another. Whenever locality is high, caching can result in significant performance benefits.

Caches often only maintain a subset of data instead of maintaining the entire data record present at the origin site. When a cache runs out of space, it needs to determine which of the older entries to discard in order to make room for new entries. Managing the space in cache can be crucial for performance when the space required at the cache is small compared to the working set of data needed by users. The working set of data is defined as the amount of data that will be accessed by the current set of active applications. When an application tends to access large objects (e.g., long video clips) it is likely that the working set may exceed the storage available at a cache. In other cases, the working set required for the applications may be smaller than the storage available at the caches. In the latter case, cache replacement policies are essentially irrelevant.

One of the most common cache replacement schemes is the classic least recently used policy, which has been used to improve computer hardware architecture for decades. It replaces the entry in the cache that was accessed least recently by any user. When all the objects in the cache have the same size, this scheme has been found to perform quite well. When the sizes of the different objects vary, replacement policies that favor replacing larger objects help for some workloads. Workloads that tend to access small objects more frequently than large objects and working sets that are larger than the cache storage capacity tend to have better performance when large objects are replaced more frequently. Replacing large objects results in making room for many small objects and eliminates objects that are less likely to be accessed in the future.

As in the case of replicated copies, requests to the cache that result in changes to the data can cause consistency problems with the data at the origin site and the data cached at other surrogate servers. Schemes must be devised to ensure that the caches are consistent with each other. Caches are primarily designed to improve systems in which the read operations are much more frequent than the write operations. In this spirit, many caching schemes prefer not to handle update operations at the cache but simply forward them to the origin server. However, an update can invalidate data cached at other surrogate servers, and suitable consistency schemes must be used to ensure that the caches are kept consistent. The different consistency schemes for caches and replicated copies are described in the next section. A more detailed description of caching in the context of web servers can be found in [36] and [37].

5.2 DATA CONSISTENCY SCHEMES

There are many schemes that can be used to maintain the consistency of data distributed across multiple sites. The choice of the correct scheme depends on the nature of the data that is replicated. Some data requires that all replicas be kept consistent at all times, other types of data may be able to tolerate a limited time window of inconsistency, and some types of data may not require consistency at all. If the data represents the balance in the checking account of a bank, then the bank may want to ensure a consistent representation of this data at all times. If the data represents the address of an individual, a scheme that ensures that the address is made consistent within a couple of days would suffice. As an example of data for which consistency is not important, consider data that is used to store a set of colors to be used for rendering. Even if the color scheme changes at the origin site, using the old scheme at the surrogate will not result in an incorrect result. Archival data, which will not changed once it is published, has no strong requirement for consistency. One must keep in mind that the consistency requirements for the similar pieces of data may depend on the environment in which they are used. A consistent color scheme may be very crucial for some environments, but may be unnecessary in others.

We consider the different types of consistency schemes that can be used for managing consistency among replicated copies of data. The first scheme that we consider is periodic synchronization, which works well for data that can tolerate a limited time window of inconsistency. The second scheme is update notification, which reduces the time window of inconsistency to the same magnitude as network latency. The third scheme covers techniques that ensure that replicated copies of data are always kept consistent with each other.

5.2.1 Periodic Synchronization

The concept of periodic synchronization is relatively simple. The multiple copies of data that are distributed in the network are synchronized with each other at periodic intervals. The synchronization may be done at regular periodic intervals, or triggered by another event that may occur at irregular intervals. As an example, synchronization of a cached data item may be done on every fifth request for that item, or even on a per-request basis, or a data item may be reretrieved from the origin server after every ten minutes.

The most common type of periodic synchronization uses "write-thru" caching. In the write-thru caching scheme, any requests that update data are forwarded to the origin site that maintains the official copy of the data. The official copy of the data is always current with all the updates. Other caches then synchronize with the official copy at periodic intervals. The synchronization with the official copy can be done by replicating at periodic intervals, or by expiring cached copies of the data. When replication is used, each surrogate site replicates the official copy of the data at periodic intervals. The replication may be triggered by each of the surrogate sites individually, or by the origin site. When expiration time is used, each surrogate site assigns an expiration time to any cached data. The cached entry expires at a fixed time period after it is cached. Expired entries are removed from the cache. If a request accesses the expired entry, it is retrieved from the official copy of the data and cached once again. Both periodic replication and expiration time ensure that any cached entries become consistent after a fixed time period.

A variant of periodic synchronization can be performed by modified "read-thru" caching. In modified read-thru caching, read requests for cached data items are validated with the origin server to check if a new copy is available. Although read-thru caching does not reduce the response time to a client when the data item being retrieved is relatively small, it can result in substantial network bandwidth savings (and the associated reduction in response time) when the data items being cached are large in size.

Another type of periodic synchronization can be done without using write-thru caching. In this scheme, each surrogate site maintains its own replicated copy of the data and performs reads/updates to the local copy of the data. At periodic intervals, the different replicas of the data are merged together to provide a consistent replica across all of the surrogate sites. The replica at each site consists of multiple data records, and each record carries a global time stamp that represents the time when the data record was updated. The global time stamp usually consists of the local time of update at the replica followed by the identity of the replica where the record is located. If the clocks on the different replicas are roughly synchronized, the global time stamp approximately represents the relative order in which the updates happened to a record. During the replication time, each data record is updated with the version that has the highest global time stamp across all the replicas. This ensures that all the replicas of the data are synchronized with each other at periodic intervals.

Periodic synchronization works very well for data that can tolerate limited windows of inconsistency. As an example, a set of addresses can each be replicated on a daily basis to make them consistent with each other. In the World Wide Web, caching surrogates use expiration time as a mechanism to cache web pages for a limited amount of time. Periodic synchronization is not suitable for data whose copies must always be kept consistent with each other.

5.2.2 Update Notification

The problem with periodic synchronization is that the window of inconsistency depends upon the synchronization period that is selected in a somewhat arbitrary fashion. In most cases, copies of data can be made consistent with each other by exchanging a few messages. Such an exchange can reduce the window of inconsistency to a small multiple of the network latency between any two sites within the CDN.

The basic idea behind update notification is that anyone noticing an update sends a message to inform all the participants in a CDN about the fact that a data record has changed. The notification can also contain information about where the most recent copy of the data can be obtained. The other participants can then synchronize their records with the updated information.

The simplest type of update notification uses write-thru caching with a single official copy of the data. The official site (typically the origin site of the CDN) keeps track of the updates and processes them in the order in which it receives them. On each update, the official site sends a notification to all of the caches informing them that the specific data record has been changed. Each site that receives the update can invalidate any local copies of the record that it may have, and retrieve the new copy from the origin server.

Many variations of the basic update notification scheme can be easily devised. Instead of sending a notification that a record has changed, the notification message can actually carry the updated record. When the data records are small, this provides for a more efficient way of notifying the CDN sites of changes. Another variation would be for the notification to be sent out by the CDN site that forwards the update request instead of the official site. This would reduce the processing required at the official site. The updates can be sent unreliably over UDP, or by using a reliable transport protocol such as TCP, and the delivery mechanism may even require that each surrogate site acknowledge that it has received and processed the notification.

If a specific data record is only cached at a few CDN sites, then notifying all of the CDN sites of changes to the record may be unnecessary. Such notifications consume network bandwidth and processing cycles at each site. In these cases, it is helpful for the site that generates the notification to maintain a list of sites that may have cached a particular record. Only those sites are informed of any updates to the specific record. The maintenance of this list is normally done by the official site along with write-thru caching. Since the official sites sees all the requests for the data record, as well as all requests for caching, it is the natural choice to maintain this list. This scheme reduces network bandwidth usage and the number of notifications received at each surrogate site, at the expense of slightly increased complexity at the origin site.

Since the number of data records is large, maintaining a list of sites for each data record can result in a very large number of lists. One way to reduce the size of lists is to define a limited set of categories. The list of sites that will receive notifications is maintained only on a per-category basis. Each record belongs to one or more of the categories defined above. When the update request for a record is received, all the sites that are listed for the appropriate category (or categories) are sent an invalidation notification along with the identity of the record. Each site can check if the invalidated record has been cached locally and if so, invalidate it. This approach provides an intermediate point between generating notifications to all of the sites for each update and maintaining a separate list for each data record.

Up to this point, we have considered data records to be independent of each other. Depending on the structure of the data, a data record may have a dependency on other records. As an example, a data record containing the total current value of a portfolio may depend on the current value of the market price of some stock symbols. In this case, a change in the stock price may cause an invalidation of several portfolio records. The dependencies among the different records can be captured by means of a dependency graph, in which each node consists of a data record and a directed edge connects a record to the other records that may depend on it. This dependency graph can then be used to determine the dependent data records. The official site can then decide to send the appropriate notification for the dependent records as well. The process can be repeated if needed.

The process of asynchronous notification works well for data records that can tolerate inconsistency windows in the order of a few tens of milliseconds (of the same order as typical network latencies on the Internet). Stock quotes [38], software distribution [70], and current scores in a sports event [39] are some examples for which update notification has been used. Note that the update notification process is not designed to guarantee consistency of the different copies of data; it simply reduces the inconsistency window. The data record is modified prior to the start of the notification process, and it is possible that due to network losses some systems may not receive the notification in time. If guaranteed data consistency is required, the schemes described in the next section should be used.

5.2.3 Consistent Updates

For data that can not tolerate any amount of inconsistency, we need to use schemes developed within distributed databases to ensure synchronization and consistency of data. Examples of such data include items such as balances in bank or trading accounts, in which inconsistency can result in serious financial penalties. The schemes developed for distributed databases ensure serialization and consistency of updates across multiple sites. The enforcement of atomicity, serialization, and consistency is often referred to as transactional semantics. A transaction could be a read or write operation on one or more data records.

Atomicity implies that a transaction should either happen or not happen at all. Serialization means that two transactions initiated across multiple sites that may be proceeding in parallel should have the same effect as if one of them was executed after another. The order in which the two transactions are performed is normally not important. Consistency means that the value of data records in all replicated copies should be the same after the transaction completes.

In a single site, atomicity and serialization are achieved via mutually exclusive locks that have to be acquired before the data is read or modified. The order in which locks are obtained determines the order in which transactions are executed. Locks may be defined at various levels of granularity—per data record, one per type of record, or over an entire database. The higher granularity increases the number of locks in the system but permits more concurrency, thereby resulting in improved user response time. The basic locking mechanism is augmented by operating system and programming language constructs such as monitors or the synchronized tag in Java programming language, which hide the basic operation of locks from most of the programmers. Consistency is a nonissue when a single site is concerned.

When we extend the concept to multiple sites with copies of the same data, atomicity, serialization, and consistency are obtained by extending the concept of locking to a distributed environment. The classical approach toward this goal is the use of the two-phase commit, a feature ubiquitously supported in distributed databases [40]. The two-phase commit protocol operates in two phases, the preparation phase and the commit phase. In the preparation phase, the originator of a request sends out a message to all of the other sites within the CDN. Each site will obtain the appropriate locks for performing the transaction, and send a positive acknowledgment back to the originator. If one of the sites is unable to obtain the lock, it will send a negative acknowledgment and the transaction will be aborted. If all the sites complete the preparation phase by sending back a positive acknowledgement, the origi-

nator will start the commit phase. In the commit phase, the originator will ask each site to perform the transaction. Each site will
complete the transaction and send back a positive acknowledgement to the originator. If the site receives positive acknowledge-
ments from all of the sites, it will ask them to release the locks as a
final step. If the site does not receive the positive acknowledge-
ments, it will ask all of the sites to roll back the transaction.

The two phase commit is a time-proven method for obtaining
consistent updates. However, the number of messages exchanged
for this type of update grows with the number of sites involved, and
the time required to do this update grows as well. While the
method performs quite well for databases connected together by a
low latency local area network, the performance degrades quickly
over wide area links. As a result, the use of two-phase commit in a
wide-area CDN must be carefully examined for performance implications.

5.3 CACHING FOR DIFFERENT TYPES OF DATA

Since the caching paradigm is the most dominant way to share
data in existing content distribution service providers, it is worthwhile to see how different types of data are typically cached within a CDN. In this section, we look at various types of data and
look at the appropriate caching schemes for those types of data.

The first type of data that we will consider is static data or data
that is not likely to change or changes very slowly. The next type of
data that we consider is dynamic data, which is data that changes
relatively frequently. The third type of data we consider is the type
that is generated by processing queries or transformation of existing data records. The fourth type of data whose caching we consider is steaming multimedia streams. The fifth and sixth types of
data we consider are examples of structured data, namely, the content of relational databases and LDAP directory servers. The final
type of data whose caching we consider are the program codes or
application logic that must run at the different CDN sites.

5.3.1 Caching Static Content

Static data is one of the easier items to cache at a surrogate site
within a CDN. A set of items that need to be cached can be

pushed by the origin site, or pulled on demand from the origin site when a request for data not in the cache is received. The currency of the cached item can be maintained by maintaining an expiration time for the cached object. If a cached item is relatively large and it is important that the most recent version be served, the cache can check with the origin site to see if the cached object has changed and retrieve the current version in case the cached version is not the same as the version at the origin site. Since static data items change relatively infrequently, a periodic synchronization scheme for managing consistency works quite well. Caching any static item can reduce the user-perceived latency if the item is likely to be accessed repeatedly from the cache. For applications with a high degree of temporal locality, caching static data on demand is likely to improve the user-perceived latency in retrieving an object. For applications with a high degree of spatial locality, it is advantageous to prefetch related data items on the first access to a data record, since applications are likely to access those data items in the subsequent requests.

5.3.2 Caching Dynamic Content

Dynamic content refers to data that can change frequently and quickly becomes outdated. Caching dynamic data helps in situations in which the data is likely to be read many times before it becomes out of date. The players' scores in a tennis match change fairly quickly, roughly at the interval of a few seconds. If the match is being watched by a global audience, e.g., Wimbledon matches, thousands of people are likely to request the score before it changes. In these cases, caching the current set of scores can be quite effective. On the other hand, if only a few reads are expected before the data changes again, it is best not to cache the data and to simply service all requests from the origin sites.

Since dynamic data changes quickly, a good approach for caching it would be to broadcast the new changed data to all of the caches as soon as it changes. With network round-trip latencies being less than a hundred milliseconds, each cache would be able to obtain the data relatively quickly, and provide it to the readers. Techniques such as dependency graphs and category-based notifications (see Section 5.2.2) can be used to further improve the efficiency of sending out the updates for this type of data.

5.3.3 Caching Processed Data

Since applications perform various types of processing on the data items, it could be advantageous in some cases to cache the results of the processing of data, rather than the raw data itself. The processing operation performed may be running a query against a set of data items or a reformatting of a data item, e.g., translating a web page from French to English. If the same processing request is expected shortly thereafter, it may be advantageous to cache the results rather than the raw data.

When the cost of processing the data is high, caching the processed data can save on repeated processing at the cache. As an example, if the English translation of an article published by a French editor is in high demand, caching the translated document can eliminate the need to do the translation for future requests. Similarly, if a search for books on the subject of "Home Improvement" is frequently observed at on-line book stores, caching the results of this search can save significant processing cycles and improve user response time.

Two facts need to be considered when deciding on a caching scheme for processed data. One is that the total possible types of processing requests, e.g., query types, are typically much larger than the typical total number of data records one may have. The other is that the same processing requests can be formulated in many different ways.

As an example, an on-line book store may have a searchable catalogue of ten thousand books. Assume that each book is characterized by four attributes, say its title, the name of author, the subject, and the ISBN number. About forty thousand queries (give or take a few duplicates) can be constructed simply by asking for an attribute and the associated value for each book. When different combinations of the basic query are considered, the number of queries becomes even larger. Furthermore, there is nothing preventing a user from constructing a query asking for an author who may not be in the catalogue. Since the number of queries that can be formulated is dependent on the values taken by the attributes of a record, they are much larger than the number of records themselves.

The other fact is that a query may be made in many different ways yet have the same answer. A simple example is two queries with an author's name and a subject, but with the attribute values enumerated in a different order. The caching system must be smart enough to recognize these variations as different forms of the same query.

The common approach used to address these concerns is to define a canonical representation of a processing request. The canonical representation could be a query expressed with the attributes enumerated in alphabetical order. The canonical representation of the query would be the same for all its variants. The canonical representation can be based on the notion of templates, which may look only at specific fields of a query in order to construct the canonical representation. This can eliminate some parts of a query that do not impact the search results, e.g., a parameter that specifies how many columns the result should be formatted in does not impact the set of data records that will result from the search.

In order to handle the large number of query types, a caching policy can be used. This consists of defining a subset of the canonical representations as queries that are worth caching. Another set of queries might be characterized as not worth caching. These caching policies help to make caching more effective.

When a query is received at the cache, the cache converts the query into a canonical representation. It then checks to see if the canonical representation matches a cached query. If so, the cached query is returned. If the query results turn out to be a subset of a cached query, the new query can be satisfied by means of extra processing on the results of the cached query. As an example, if a cached query looked for all books by the author Verma, and a new query looking for the books by author Verma and the subject "Content Distribution Networks" is received, the new query can be satisfied by running the results on the previously cached results.

With some types of data processing requests, the processing results in creating multiple versions of the same data item. As an example, a processing request may translate a file into one of five different languages, or may convert an image into versions with differing resolutions. In these cases, it is easier to cache one or more variants of the data in the local cache, and use the same techniques as that for caching the original data item. The multiple variants of the same data item can be created when first needed.

5.3.4 Caching Multimedia Streams

Multimedia content consists of audio-visual data that can be used by a client in one of two ways. The entire multimedia file can be downloaded by the client and then played from the local disk. However, for long files, this can result in a large waiting period while the file is downloaded. In order to reduce the waiting time before one can play the multimedia file, the so-called streaming mode is used. In the steaming mode, the client starts playing the clip as soon as it has downloaded a segment of the file for a fixed period of time (say 1 second). While the currently downloaded segment is being played, other segments are loaded from the network to be played when the current segment finishes playing. In order to interoperate, the client and server need to conform to a common streaming protocol. Two commonly used protocols are defined by Real Networks [41] and a standard such as MPEG [42].

The caching of multimedia files that are downloaded completely and played in the batch mode is similar to caching static objects, except that the objects would tend to be much larger in size. For the caching of streaming multimedia streams, the surrogate cache has to implement the function of the streaming server. The surrogate cache can also make caching decisions on the granularity of a segment of the multimedia file rather than the entire file. For multimedia files that are in high demand, all the segments can be kept in the cache. For multimedia files that are less likely to be accessed, the cache can only keep the initial few segments, and download the remaining ones on demand when a client actually accesses them. This can greatly reduce the storage requirements at the surrogate cache.

Some steaming servers allow support for varying quality of service streaming to different clients. Clients on a dial-up connection will get a lower bandwidth stream. The lower bandwidth is obtained either by reducing the resolution of the graphic frames included in the stream or by skipping a few frames. In these cases, the relative demands for the different qualities of service can also be used to determine which segments of a multimedia file or which versions of a segment ought to be stored at a cache [43]

5.3.5 Caching Database Entries

A database is a repository of multiple data items with a structure. The most prevalent databases at the time of the writing of this book are relational databases. A relational database organizes information into one or more tables, and each table contains a fixed number of columns. Each entry in the database is defined by a row of the table. Information in the relational database is accessed using a query language, which is almost always SQL[40]. SQL is a complex language that allows the selection of a subset of the entries in the database using a sophisticated set of expressions, including loops and if-conditional statements.

Although distributed databases have been around for a while, they do not perform that well due to the need to maintain a consistent update operation. The alternative approach, in which some databases are cached copies of the original master, has attracted some attention in recent years. As a database cache, the cache would normally process only queries that do not modify the entries in the database.

One approach to building a database cache is to use query result caching as discussed above. Query result caching can be an effective method that can be built into the access protocol accessing a database. However, the complexity of SQL statements implies that a canonical representation of the queries for all SQL queries may be difficult to achieve. However, for a limited subset of queries (e.g., the subset of SQL doing searches on a simple Boolean expression of attribute–value pairs), query result caching can be done in a relatively simple manner. For applications in which simple queries predominate, query result caching for databases can prove quite effective in a wide area CDN environment.

An alternative to query result caching is to cache a subset of the database records at the surrogate sites and run SQL operations against the local subset of data. Updates are forwarded to the origin site database. One can define the subset of data that can be cached at the database. This subset can be defined as a set of tables, a set of tables with selected columns, or as some other subset or chunk of the database [44]. Each SQL query also needs to be analyzed to validate that the results can be obtained correctly on the basis of the cache data. Updates to the origin database need to be propagated to the cached copies as quickly as possible, e.g., using a reliable version of update notification, to minimize the possibility of an inconsistency between the cached copy of data and the original database.

The key challenge in database caching is to maintain the highly reliable and consistent database transactional semantics without affecting performance. As discussed earlier, transactional semantics are at odds with performance acceleration using distribution.

Defining the subset of database entries that can be cached is a way of capturing application-specific information about those tables/columns for which the application access pattern does not require strict transactional semantics, and thus gain performance by compromising on the strict consistency of cached data.

5.3.6   Caching LDAP Directories

An LDAP [45] directory is another type of organized data. Like a relational database, an LDAP directory consists of a set of tables with a specific set of columns. The different types of tables and their constituent columns are defined by the schema that is used by an LDAP directory. As compared to a database, LDAP directory has two key differences: (1) all its entries are organized in a hierarchical manner using a distinguishing name for each entry and (2) LDAP access allows for a very simple set of query and lookup operations. A lookup, addition, or modification requires specifying the distinguishing name of the record being worked on. The search can only be composed of simple filters with binary operators between an attribute and the value it is allowed/not allowed to have. Furthermore, LDAP traditionally has been used for applications in which data tends to be relatively static. These characteristics make data stored in LDAP directories a primary target for caching at surrogate sites. As in the other examples in this section, we assume that modification requests are forwarded to the origin site, and that an appropriate consistency mechanism is used for ensuring data consistency.

The two basic approaches that can be used for caching LDAP data are query result caching and caching a selected subset of data. With query result caching, one translates the LDAP requests (lookups or searches) into a canonical representation. LDAP lookup results specify the distinguishing name of the object they are looking up, and it is relatively simple to check if the named object is already cached locally. LDAP search requests require a pointer to the data hierarchy that is to be searched, and a Boolean expression that identifies the attributes being looked for. Each subcomponent of the Boolean expression specifies the value of attributes being looked for. An example of the LDAP search query could be: look up all objects under the hierarchy identified by the distinguishing name "organization=IBM," where the attribute class type is employee and the attribute age is less than

40. This example consists of a conjunction (and-ing) of three basic attribute–operation–value combinations.

Boolean expressions can be readily converted into canonical forms, the two most prevalent ones being the conjunctive normal form and the disjunctive normal form. The former consists of a conjunction (and-ing) of many subexpressions, where each subexpression is a disjunction (or-ing) of basic terms (or attribute–operation–value combinations for LDAP). The latter consists of a disjunction of many subexpressions, where each subexpression is a conjunction of basic terms.

Such canonical representations allow LDAP query results to be cached and run in a relatively simple manner, since it is relatively straightforward to determine if a new request can be satisfied from the results of a previous request. If the conjunctive normal form is used as the canonical format, a query can be satisfied from the results of any prior query where a subset of the subexpressions of the current query is present. If the disjunctive normal form is used as the canonical format, a query can be satisfied from the results of any prior query where a superset of the subexpressions of the current query is present.

The other alternative for caching LDAP queries is to cache a subset of the data that is present in the origin directory. This approach is similar to that of caching specific subsets of data in a database. In the context of LDAP, it is easier to define the subset as a branch of the hierarchical structure imposed by the distinguished naming hierarchy. Since both searches and lookups identify the part of the naming hierarchy they are to be performed on, maintaining subsets of data in a hierarchical manner leads to a quick decision as to whether a specific request can be satisfied locally or not.

5.3.7   Caching Application Code

Just as passive data elements are cached at surrogate sites that constitute a CDN, the program part or code can also be cached at the surrogate site to enable some of the processing functions to be performed there. The programs that are executed to fulfill requests from the users of an application have the characteristic that they change relatively slowly. This implies that much of the application processing that happens at the origin site can also be offloaded and executed at the surrogate site of a CDN.

Some of the processing that is involved in the formatting and reading of information in a specific way can easily be executed at the edge server. In many CDN sites, the type of processing that can be performed is determined by an a priori configuration and installation of the appropriate software. However, the advent of mobile code technology, such as Java applets, mobile agents, and active networks implies that the distribution of processing capabilities can be done on demand or via configuration at an application back-end. An example of this capability, IBM WebSphere Edge Server, offers the ability to offload portions of an application to be executed at a cache by configuration from the origin site.

An application code can be retrieved and cached by loading programs on demand from the origin server, or by pushing the appropriate software modules from the origin site. IBM Edge Server follows the latter model, but the former model can be used by extending network class loaders found in languages such as Java to retrieve code from the origin server, as well as any initialization parameters that may be needed for executing the code.

Caching of application programs enables distributed program execution with a single point where software is installed and configured. However, the executing programs may result in exceptions or errors, and the resulting error messages, as well as any other output produced by the programs, needs to be channeled back to the originating site so that they can be analyzed.

5.4 CACHING IN CDNs FOR WEB SERVERS

As an example of a common application that can be used in content distribution networks, let us look at some examples of the above type of caching in the context of web servers. For the purposes of this discussion, we assume that the web server at the origin site consists of three tiers. The first tier is the HTTP daemon (or the traditional web server), the second tier provides an environment for execution of dynamic programs (e.g., Java servlets or cgi-bin scripts), and the third tier is a database that is used to store any data needed for the web server. Any requests for static content or images are serviced by the first tier. Any request that requires some amount of processing is serviced by the second tier, which may access the third tier in order to obtain the data necessary for its storage.

The information at the origin site may be offloaded to the CDN sites in varying proportions. We will consider the various cases in which more of the processing at each tier is moved into the surrogate sites of the CDN.

The initial content that can be moved with relative ease to the surrogate site are static images and selected HTML pages. These pages can be offloaded to the surrogate site using one of the many client redirection techniques described in Chapter 3. Let us consider the case where the clients are rerouted by modifying the HTML pages at the websites in conjunction with domain-name-server-based techniques. If the origin site is www.company.com and it is desired to offload the serving of the image at the original URL or www.company.com/images/img1.gif, all occurrences of this link in the HTML content of the site are changed to the URL edge.company.com/images/img1.gif. A modified domain name server then directs requests for the machine edge.company.com to one of the many CDN surrogate sites. The same technique can be used for HTML pages.

When the request for the image or HTML file is received at the edge, it determines which original URL the request pertained to. In the example above, this can be done by a simple manipulation of the name of the machine being accessed in the URL. The surrogate site needs to have a caching web surrogate that can serve the appropriate content from its local cache, or retrieve it from the origin server if it is not found in the local cache.

A web server performs other functions than simply serving static pages. One of the common functions provided by a web server is the processing of macros (such as server-side "include" directives) that are included in a page. A server-side include consists of tags that are replaced by the web server with the results of executing specific programs. An example of a server side include is a tag that expands into the current time of day as measured at the server. If the web server at the CDN surrogate site understands the semantics of the server-side includes that are provided by the content at the origin site, the surrogate site can do a similar expansion of the tags on the cached static content.

A more sophisticated form of caching can be provided at the CDN surrogate sites by employing the concepts of query result caching (caching processed data). Requests to invoke cgi-bin scripts or Java servlets are directed to the surrogate sites. The surrogate site checks its local cache to see if it has a cached query result that can provide the desired information. If not, the query is forwarded to the origin site and the results cached to service similar future requests.

At the next level, more complex functions traditionally performed at the second tier can be moved into the CDN surrogate site. Many web servers offer the capability to translate pages into one or more languages, depending on the preference selected by a user. Such a translation can be done by means of a Java servlet (or a cgi-bin program) executing at the CDN surrogate site. Another type of function commonly performed by the servlet/cgi-bin is assembling of multiple fragments into a single HTML page. A web page demonstrating the current scores in an event like the Olympics consists of several portions of data that are joined together. Each piece of data includes the current score in a specific sports event. A composition servlet at the surrogate site can assemble the different fragments together; an update notification system then sends out the current set of scores to all of the surrogates at the site.

The previous paragraph discussed the execution of a fixed set of servlets by the CDN surrogate site. At the next level, the servlet programs can be loaded dynamically from the origin website. This would allow the origin site to execute any servlet at the CDN surrogate site. Servlet programs that require large numbers of computational cycles but do not need access to the data in the third tier frequently can benefit from this architecture. One of the advantages of having the programs downloaded dynamically (application caching) is that the surrogate sites can have a standard configuration, and new applications can be deployed simply by configuring them at the origin site.

At the next level of the offload capability, portions of the database can be cached at the CDN surrogate sites. This moves the third tier of the web servers into the CDN surrogate site. A larger number of programs can now be executed at the surrogate sites. One nice feature of caching databases and the third tier structure at the surrogate site is that the second tier applications, which are more complex and numerous, do not need to be modified to ensure that they can run effectively at the edge.

In Chapter 7, we look at several web-based applications, and how they can be made to run efficiently in a CDN environment using various types of caching.

6 Interconnecting the CDN Sites

The CDN network consists of many surrogate sites that cooperate in order to service a common application or set of applications. As part of this cooperation, the different CDN sites need to communicate with each other. In this chapter, we look at the different types of interconnection schemes that can be deployed within the CDN sites. The primary communication in a CDN site is likely to be between a surrogate site and the origin site, but surrogate-to-surrogate communication is also possible in many situations.

When a surrogate site is unable to satisfy a client's request because the requisite data is not available in the local cache, it needs to communicate with the origin site to receive it. A surrogate site to origin site communication also happens when notifications are sent by the origin site, or data is pushed to the cache by the origin site. The quality of connectivity between the surrogate site and the origin site can have a significant impact on the performance of the CDN. In this chapter, we look at the different schemes that can be used to improve the connectivity between the sites that make up a CDN.

Since the clients need to communicate with the origin site as well as some of the surrogate sites, there must exist a shared network that connects the clients to the different sites within the CDN. We refer to this shared network as the common network. The common network offers connectivity between the different sites of a CDN, but the performance of this path may not be very good. Since the performance gain of a CDN is obtained by having surrogates located close to the clients, the path on the common network between the surrogate and the origin site is likely to be as congested as the path between the client and the network. A better performance gain can be obtained if the connectivity between the surrogate site and the origin site is better than that available through the common network.

127

The simplest way to obtain a better performing link between the surrogate sites and the origin sites is to create a secondary network that interconnects the different sites in the CDN. Although operating a secondary network has certain costs associated with it, this approach can result in a very fast private network between the sites of the CDN. In the first section of this chapter, we look at the different types of private interconnection that can be used between the surrogate sites and the client sites.

In many cases, operating a private secondary network is not a cost-effective option. However, since the communication between the CDN sites occurs between two cooperating sites, one can design techniques that can result in a more efficient communication even on the common network. By using a collaborative communication protocol between the surrogate site and the origin site, one can obtain higher throughput on the common network than provided by the standard communication protocols used between a client and the origin server. The second section of this chapter discusses the options that can be used to squeeze better performance out of the common network.

The third section of this chapter examines the multicast communication protocols that can be used to efficiently distribute and replicate the content between the different sites that make up the CDN. The final section deals with management issues that need to be considered when interconnecting the different CDN sites. These include issues related to user tracking, usage monitoring, accounting, and systems administration and management.

6.1   USING A SECONDARY NETWORK

The best connectivity between the sites that make up a CDN is obtained when one can run a private network connecting the different sites within the CDN. Having a private network infrastructure leads to better performance for two reasons: (1) if the budget permits, it is possible to have links connecting surrogate sites to the origin site that are faster than those connecting the clients to the origin site; (2) there is no competing traffic from extraneous sources on the private network.

Such a private network can be created as a wired network or by using wireless communication techniques such as those based on satellites. The issues involved in both types of networks are discussed in the following subsections.

6.1.1 Wired Secondary Networks

Having a private line between a surrogate server and the origin site would be an ideal way (except for the issue of cost) to connect the surrogate sites to the origin sites within a CDN. The capacity of the private line can be selected to be faster than the capacity normally available between the surrogate and the server on the common network. The delays incurred in the communication between the surrogate and the origin site on the private network are also likely to be smaller than those on the common network.

While it may appear counterintuitive that the latency on the private network between two points is lower than the latency between the same points on the common network, it must be kept in mind that the physical distance between two points on the common network is often not the primary cause of the latency between two sites. Most latency is due to the processing delays in different routers and switches that constitute the path between the two sites on the network. Thus, an alternative path that can connect the two sites using a fewer number of hops can actually result in lower latency.

In the context of the Internet, another way to obtain better connectivity between two sites is to obtain connectivity at both sites with the same ISP. The Internet is a loose conglomeration of many independently operated ISP networks. The connectivity across two ISP networks comes without any assurances regarding the performance of this connectivity. However, the ISPs often provide assurances on the performance (in the form of performance SLAs) of their individual networks to their customers [46]. The use of a common shared ISP can improve the performance of the link between two sites.

The technique of sharing a common ISP can also be used to advantage by operators of websites (and CDN surrogate sites) that are to be accessed by independent users over the Internet. If a site has connectivity to multiple ISP networks, then its connectivity to all the customers on that ISP is likely to be much improved. As a result, many websites choose to have connectivity with multiple ISPs. This provides faster access to the site, and also provides a fail-safe mechanism in case one of the ISPs experiences a fault.

6.1.2 Wireless Secondary Networks

An alternative to a wired secondary network is to have a wireless secondary network between the different sites. The wireless network could be a satellite network or made up of a radio links, depending on the physical separation between the different sites of the network. A satellite network uses a geo-stationary satellite in the sky as an intermediate router. Each site sends data to the satellite, which relays it toward the desired target. Radio links are established along direct lines of sight between the sites, and can only be used if the different sites are relatively close together. A wireless network may turn out to be a viable option when some of the content distribution sites are in remote locations without good connectivity. Such locations include the mountain regions of the United States and many parts of Africa and Asia where the infrastructure for wired connectivity is relatively underdeveloped.

A wireless secondary network typically would not have the same characteristics as a wired network. A satellite network typically has larger latencies than the wired network due to the need for each transmission to go through a satellite. Similarly, the loss rates of the wireless links are much higher than fiber-optical wires. As a result, a wireless secondary infrastructure is not likely to perform better than the corresponding wired infrastructure. In some cases, the wireless link between two sites may even have worse performance than the corresponding connection over the common network.

Despite this drawback, a satellite-based wireless secondary network has a fundamental advantage over the wired infrastructure when it comes to multicast communication. The satellite-based infrastructure allows a site to send the same data to all of the receivers at the same time. The data relayed by the satellite can be received and processed by all of the sites simultaneously. Thus, if the intersite communication among the different surrogate sites happened to be predominantly of a multicast nature, a satellite infrastructure would be very effective.

Much of the communication that occurs among the CDN sites is multicast in nature. When caches at the surrogate sites need to be prepopulated with data that is likely to be addressed, the data needs to be multicast to all of the sites. When a piece of data is updated, the invalidation notification needs to reach all of the caches. When replicating the content on a periodic basis, the contents of the origin site need to be sent to all of the surrogate sites.

In a CDN that uses any of these techniques for managing its caches, a wireless satellite network might provide a good solution for a secondary network.

6.2 OPTIMIZATIONS ON THE COMMON NETWORK

In many cases, a secondary private network is not viable due to cost reasons. Operating a secondary network is expensive, and any performance gains obtained by operating a private network may not be worth the price. In this case, one needs to develop a scheme that will improve the communication quality between two sites participating in a CDN. In this section, we look at some of the techniques that can enable such efficient communication.

Since the sites in the CDN are going over the common network, they have access to the same physical resources as the rest of entities using the common network. However, since the sites know that they are only communicating with themselves, they can cooperate to exploit the resources in a more efficient manner. The communication between the clients and the CDN sites has to occur using the standard protocols that operate on the common network. Within the Internet, each CDN site must communicate using the standard TCP or UDP protocols. However, when the sites that constitute the CDN need to communicate with each other, they can use a private protocol that is more efficient than the standard protocols.

To examine some of the private protocols that can be used, we will concentrate on the Internet, where standard communication occurs using the TCP/IP protocol suite. The application level protocol that operates atop these protocols varies depending on the application. Optimizations can be obtained by modifying any protocol above the transport layer. The transport layer is the first layer that is interpreted only by the endpoints of the communication, and not by routers in the middle of the network.

6.2.1 Private Transport Protocols

The bulk of traffic that is carried on the Internet and enterprise intranets consists of TCP traffic. The TCP protocol is a time-tested protocol that has proved to be stable and fair under a wide variety of network conditions. For connections that exchange a significant amount of data, the performance of TCP is strongly influenced by its congestion control scheme. For connections that exchange a small amount of data, the performance of TCP is influenced strongly by the time required to establish a connection.

6.2.1.1 TCP Performance

The performance of TCP is influenced by its connection establishment time, its flow control scheme, and its congestion control scheme. Flow control refers to schemes designed to ensure that the sender of data does not overflow the buffers available at a receiver. Congestion control refers to schemes designed to ensure that no intermediate node on the path between the sender and the receiver is congested (i.e., overflowing its buffers for packet forwarding).

For applications that exchange significant amounts of data, TCP flow control and congestion control schemes are the primary determinant of the throughput that can be obtained in the data exchange. For downloading web pages containing large graphics, or in large file transfers, the congestion control can be expected to have a significant impact on the performance.

For applications that exchange a small amount of data (e.g., data that is less than one TCP segment), congestion control performance is not the key bottleneck. The key determinant of their performance is the time required by TCP to establish a connection. The connection establishment time takes at least one round trip and data transmission cannot begin until the connection is established.

TCP is a reliable protocol that sends data in units called TCP segments. The receiver sends an acknowledgment to the sender for each segment that it receives. If a sender does not receive an acknowledgment after a time-out period, it knows that a loss has occurred. If an acknowledgment is received, the sender knows that the packet has gotten through.

In TCP flow control, the endpoints of communications exchange information about the size of the receive buffers they have for each connection. The sender will never have more data in-flight (i.e., data that has been sent but not acknowledged by the receiver) than the size of the receiver's buffer. This limit on the amount of data in-flight is called the receiver window.

TCP congestion control provides another limit on the amount of in-flight data. This limit is called the congestion window. Since the receiver will never run out of buffer space, any loss in the network is assumed to be from a congested router along the route. When a loss occurs, the congestion window is reduced, and when packets are getting through, the congestion window is increased. The effective rate is obtained by dividing the congestion window by the average round-trip time between the sender and the receiver.

The TCP congestion protocol operates in two modes. When a new connection is established, it starts with an initial window size. The window size is incremented by a segment every time an acknowledgment is received. This has the effect of doubling the congestion window every round-trip time. After a certain number of these steps, the window size is incremented by a fraction of the segment, resulting in a linear increase of the window size. If a loss is detected, the window size is reduced by half.

In order to improve the effective performance of TCP applications, we need to develop schemes that will work around the constraints imposed by the protocol.

6.2.1.2 Sharing a TCP Connection

If the communication between the different CDN sites consists of several exchanges of small amounts of data, they can gain in performance by reusing a TCP connection across the different exchanges. Instead of establishing several TCP connections, one for each exchange, they can establish a single connection, and thus pay the overhead of connection establishment only once across all the exchanges. This would reduce the time needed to complete each exchange.

As an example, consider the case of a CDN in which the surrogate sites are acting as HTTP surrogate servers. The surrogate server provides access to multiple clients. It can establish a different connection for every client request that is not available in the cache, disconnecting the connection to the origin site whenever the client disconnects from the surrogate. However, if the files being retrieved are small, the surrogate may gain in performance by maintaining this connection. When a new client establishes a connection with the surrogate server, its requests can be sent on the preexisting connection and the connection establishment overhead can be avoided.

The sharing of the TCP connection implies that both sites of the

CDN use a common application layer multiplexing scheme that can tunnel multiple requests onto a single TCP connection. Both sides of the communication have to conform to a common scheme so that the multiplexing operation works properly.

6.2.1.3 Multiple Concurrent TCP Connections

For communications that exchange larger amounts of data, the connection establishment overhead is not the bottleneck. The performance of the connection is impacted by the rate limits that come into play due to the congestion control and flow control schemes used by TCP.

If the amount of data in-flight is constrained by the limit on the receiver's buffer at the receiving end, then more data in-flight can be sent by using two or more parallel sessions between the two endpoints. Normally, each connection has a separate pool of receiver buffers, and a parallel session in these cases can double the effective amount of data in-flight.

If you are willing to modify the TCP software at each CDN site, a cleaner way to obtain the same effect is to increase the size of receiver buffer that is used by TCP in its connection establishment. However, it will double the receiver buffer for all TCP connections, not just those between the CDN sites. A slightly more complex option would be to selectively choose the receiver's buffer size depending on the IP address of the node that originates the connection. This option requires access to the kernel of the sites that will be communicating. If this access is not available, (e.g., if your site runs on a standard Windows platform on which TCP code cannot be modified easily), using multiple concurrent TCP connections requires only application layer modifications.

When the communication between two CDN sites is poor because of congestion on the route between the two sites, operating multiple TCP connections in parallel can also help in some cases. If there are multiple TCP flows through a congested link, and each of them implements the same congestion control scheme and has about the same round-trip time, each flow would end up with its fair share of the bandwidth at the congested link. If a pair of communicating entities choose to have multiple concurrent TCP connections instead of one, then this pair will end up with a larger fraction of the congested link and thus have a better throughput.

There are two caveats that must be considered when using multiple connections to get more than the fair share of bandwidth for the communication between the CDN sites. The first caveat is that the congestion on the link should not result from the communication between the CDN sites. If the congestion is due to the traffic between the CDN sites, the flows between the CDN sites dominate, and increasing the number of flows on each communication reduces the bandwidth share allocated to each link. As an example, consider the case where the only communication on the congested link is due to the TCP flows between two CDN sites. If only one TCP connection is used between the sites, it will open its congestion window until it is utilizing the full bandwidth of the link. If two TCP connections are used, each connection will get half of the bandwidth, and the effective throughput among the two will not increase. The result can even be worse than for a single connection because of the overhead involved in managing extra connections at the endpoints. On the other hand, if the connection between the two CDN sites is only one out of a hundred flows through the congested link, then increasing the number of flows to five allows it to get a 5/104 fraction of the link bandwidth (approximately 4.8%) as opposed to only 1% with one traffic flow.

The second caveat is that if everyone on the network starts to use a similar scheme, the resulting overall performance of the common network will be adversely impacted.

6.2.1.4 *Modified Congestion Control Schemes*
TCP is a very polite protocol wherein each sender cuts down its sending rate so as to reduce the congestion on the network. However, the participants in a CDN site can use their own congestion control protocol, which may be more aggressive than TCP. If the effective throughput of the modified congestion protocol is better than what TCP can provide, communication between the CDN sites will improve significantly.

The most aggressive thing a sender can do is to eliminate the congestion control. This implies ignoring the congestion window and sending the packets at the maximum rate that is permitted by the receiver window of flow control. If there are no congested routers along the path, there is no damage done, since the normal TCP congestion control will also speed up to this rate eventually. If there is a congested node, then packet losses will occur. Other connections, which are being polite, will cut back on their congestion window, whereas the aggressive sender will still be sending at the maximum possible rate and obtain a better performance from the network. The downside is that the network will be much worse for the polite senders who are complying with TCP.

This scheme will work only if the number of aggressive senders is negligible. If the number of aggressive senders becomes large, the entire network will be overwhelmed by the lack of congestion control. Also, if the aggressive senders are generating significant amounts of traffic on the network, they can cause more congestion and losses would have resulted from all senders complying with TCP. Not using congestion control is unsocial behavior, like cutting into the front of a queue at a restaurant. If only a few people are doing this, they get reduced waiting time at the expense of others. But if everyone starts jumping ahead in the queue, there is chaos, and much worse waiting time for everyone than if everyone followed the rules.

In order to avoid these problems, the CDN sites need to implement a congestion control scheme. One approach is to modify the congestion control scheme of TCP to become slightly more aggressive. There are many ways to do this. One can increase the number of steps in the initial phase, in which the window size is doubling every round-trip time. One can increase the size by which the window is incremented at each step. Another option is to reduce the window by merely a third instead of halving it when a loss occurs. All these adaptations will allow the sender to obtain a larger share of the network bandwidth than with the normal application. One crucial requirement is that the congestion control scheme must avoid congestion if all the senders follow the aggressive approach.

Another option is to use a rate-based congestion control mechanism. In the rate-based congestion control mechanism, the sender determines a rate at which it can send data, and will only send below that rate. The right rate of sending is determined by examining the network at the time of connection establishment, and the rate limit can be varied over time. Descriptions and analyses of several rate-based congestion control schemes can be found in the literature (see [47] or [69] for some examples).

The modified congestion control scheme must be designed with caution. The modified scheme must not be so aggressive so as to impact normal TCP connections tremendously. If the scheme is too aggressive, machines with normal TCP connections in their environment will experience serious degradation when the new congestion control scheme is used for a selected set of machines or applications. If you expect to run some of the normal applications for your own work, it would be a good idea to let them function with reasonable performance. Otherwise, many normal operations between the CDN sites could be adversely impacted.

In most cases, implementation of the modified congestion control would require changing the transport protocol implementation in the operating system kernel of the machine. Another alternative is to implement a full transport layer protocol with the modified congestion control protocol on top of UDP, or over raw IP sockets. As long as both end-points of the connection were using the same protocol, they could extract better performance from the network than normal a TCP communication would. The common implementations of voice and video transport over IP networks run over UDP instead of TCP, and implement their own rate control schemes, which are substantially different from that of TCP.

6.2.2 Coding and Content Adaptation

One way to obtain a better performance from the network is to modify the data being carried on the common network so that it can be transmitted more efficiently. By modifying the data so that it can be transmitted more efficiently, one can achieve better performance on a somewhat poor network. The basic idea is to trade off the network bandwidth needed with more processing cycles on the two end hosts.

One of the basic things that one can do to improve communication performance is to compress all the data that is being sent over the network. When a large amount of data needs to be transferred, compressing it can significantly reduce the time required for the task. On a shared network that has low bandwidth links, compression can prove to be quite useful.

Compression is an example of the changes that can be made to data that preserve its semantics while reducing its size. For some types of data, other types of changes are possible that can reduce the size of data while maintaining its semantics reasonably well. These can be considered lossy compression schemes. They can be used on graphics, images, audio, and video data to reduce their bandwidth requirements. In most cases, there is a trade-off between the amount of loss of data and the amount of bandwidth, and the CDN sites can adapt the rate at which they compress the data according to the bandwidth available on the network.

If the problem with the shared network is loss rates rather than low bandwidth, one must design schemes that will be more resilient to loss of packets. One way to obtain this goal is to transmit information so that meaningful data can be created even when some of the packets transmitted along the network are lost. The most prevalent way to do this is by the use of forward error correction (FEC) codes.

One of the ways to use FEC is to split streams of data into fixed-size bundles. Each bundle consists of several packets, and each packet is of a fixed length. The data is then written into a tabular format in which each row consists of a packet and each column consists of bytes from the packets, i.e., the first column consists of the first byte of all the packets, the second column consists of the second byte of all packets, and so on. Each element of this table consists of a byte. A function is applied to each row to create one or more additional column entries that will serve as the FEC bytes in each packet. The simplest example of such a function is XOR-ing the individual bytes to get one FEC byte, but more sophisticated functions are available that are more effective [48–51]. A function is also applied to each column to generate one or more additional rows. FEC bytes are generated for these rows, and the new rows are the FEC packets. When transmitting the data, the boundaries of the bundles need to be demarcated in the header that goes with these packets.

The inclusion of FEC bytes and FEC packets enables a receiver to reconstruct the original packets in the presence of many types of errors, e.g., errors in a few bits of the packet, the loss of a byte, or even the loss of an entire packet.

FEC codes are used in transmission of packets over unreliable media, such as IP over television signal vertical blanking interval (VBI). The vertical blanking interval is the time period in which a television screen moves from one line of the screen to the other, and can be used to transfer information. The FEC scheme used in IP over VBI use a bundle of with 14 data packets and 2 FEC packets, with each packet consisting of 14 data bytes and 2 FEC bytes. Further details of the algorithms used for computing the FEC functions and recovering from lost errors can be found in RFC 2728 [48]. FEC is also used for transferring data reliably to many receivers simultaneously in an efficient manner [48].

When using an FEC code, the sender may use a fixed scheme for generating the FEC bytes or codes in all the bundles, or feedback from the receiver to generate FEC codes only when needed. An example of the former approach is IP over VBI, in which there is no feedback from the receiver to the sender. When feedback is possible, the sender only sends the data packets (and no FEC packets or FEC bytes) in the initial transmission. When the receiver informs the sender about any packets that are incorrectly received, the sender transmits the FEC codes that would enable the receiver to reconstruct the data packet. When the loss rates are moderate, the reactive scheme will not transmit FEC packets for the majority of cases in which packets are received correctly, and save on the bandwidth.

The use of FEC requires computing the FEC packets and/or FEC bytes in bundles. This adds to the overall latency in sending data, and is suitable for bulk data transfer. This would be a good scheme to preload CDN surrogate caches over a lossy network. For interactive data, the additional latencies will render this scheme relatively unattractive.

6.3 MULTICASTING IN CDN SITES

In many cases, communication between the CDN sites consists of broadcasting data from the origin site to the surrogate sites. When caches at the surrogate sites need to be preloaded, or periodic replication needs to be take place, a large amount of data flows from the origin site to the surrogate sites. If the surrogate sites are implementing a variant of cooperating caching, they may flow a multicast query looking for any file that is not present in a cache. Therefore, a significant part of communication in a CDN site consists of broadcasting messages to the many participants in the site. In this section, we look at the different options for multicasting that can be used in a CDN.

If the underlying network infrastructure permits multicast communication, that would be the best option to use for multicasting information among the different sites. If there is no native multicast support, an equivalent capability needs to be built for efficient communication between the CDN sites. Since we are focusing on IP networks, we will examine the multicast capability available on an IP network, and how they can be used for CDN communication. The following section discusses approaches that can be made to work when IP multicast is not available.

6.3.1 IP Multicast for Overlay Interconnection

The IP standards provide for special multicast group addresses that represent multiple receiving machines. A packet sent to the multicast address reaches all the machines in the group. Machines may choose to be members of one or more multicast groups. The joining and leaving of hosts in these groups is dynamic, done by means of the Internet Group Management Protocol (IGMP) [74].

Routers in the network that support IGMP act as servers that are contacted by end nodes to join or receive the groups. All IGMP-capable routers communicate with each other to maintain the list of current members in each group, and to form a multicast routing table to route messages to all the different participants in the group. The routing tables together define one or more distribution trees connecting all members of a receiver group. The distribution tree eliminates cycles in the network, and avoids the looping of packets. A single distribution tree may be defined for all members of a multicast group, or the distribution tree may differ depending on where a packet is coming from. A variety of routing schemes have been proposed to maintain the routing tables for multicast receivers. Common routing schemes include the Distance Vector Multicast Routing Protocol (DVMRP), [52] multicast OSPF [53], and Protocol Independent Multicast (PIM) [54].

In order to exploit IP multicast, the CDN sites need to have a private multicast address that they use. All CDN sites use the multicast group to send information to all of the participants. The network takes care of routing the packets to the destinations. IP multicast works well for sending data that can tolerate a limited level of loss. However, when data needs to be transferred reliably, one needs a reliable transport protocol that can recover from network losses.

A reliable multicast protocol allows a single sender to reliably send data to more than one receiver. The fact that the sender is interacting with more than one receiver makes multicast more complex than unicast (single sender–single receiver) protocols such as TCP. Some key components of a reliable transport protocol are loss recovery, congestion control, and flow control.

Loss recovery can be obtained by two means: using FEC encoding or by having the sender retransmit the missing packets. In symmetric networks in which loss rates are low or moderate, retransmission is more efficient than FEC encoding; a combination of the two can also be used. Losses are indicated by receivers generating positive or negative acknowledgments to the senders. Loss recovery can be driven by the sender or the receiver. When driven by the sender, the sender assumes by default that receivers have only obtained data if they send an acknowledgment. When driven by the receiver, the sender assumes by default that each receiver has obtained the data. It is the receiver's responsibility to ensure that it has received all of the data. The receiver will ask the sender to retransmit any data it has not received, and can identify lost data by looking for gaps in sequence numbers of data that it actually receives.

Congestion control causes rate or sending window adaptation that is similar to that of unicast protocols. However, the level of congestion existing along the paths to different receivers would likely be different. The multicast transport protocol has to choose a sending rate or a window that accommodates all the different receivers. One option is to use the congestion information on the worst link, but this will degrade performance to all of the receivers. Another option is to split the receivers into two or more groups, each group consisting of receivers in which the congestion control information is somewhat the same. Much of the complexity in multicast congestion control lies in dividing nodes into the different groups when the congestion information changes.

Flow control information from multiple receivers is also combined in the same manner. However, since flow control information is normally obtained during only the connection establishment time, it is easier to manage than the congestion control information. Once again, the sender can decide whether to use the most constraining flow control information, or to split the receivers into multiple groups, with each group containing members with similar flow control requirements.

The IETF standards groups are working on a common, reliable multicast transport protocol [55]. Until such a standard transport protocol is available as ubiquitously as TCP, one will have to design reliable multicast transport protocols as needed for multicasting data.

6.3.2 Application Layer Overlays

One of the issues with IP multicast is that it is not always available. Forwarding multicast packets is a more complex operation for a router than forwarding unicast packets. The Internet group management protocols also create a substantial amount of traffic on the network. Due to performance concerns, many network operators turn off multicast within their network. If your CDN is running in such an environment, you need to develop schemes that will mimic multicasting, except that mulitcast is implemented within the CDN nodes themselves.

One simple scheme for multicasting in this environment is for the sender to establish a unicast connection with each of the receivers, and to send messages to each person individually. When each site of the CDN needs to communicate with each other, this approach will require $O(n^2)$ overlay links, where n is the number of sites in the CDN. When the number of receivers is small, multiple individual transmissions are the best approach. However, when the number of receives is large, it becomes slow and expensive to maintain direct connectivity among all of the nodes. The approach in application layer multicast is to use a subset of the links required for full connectivity, and to relay messages along those overlay links.

In application layer multicast, each pair of participating nodes communicates using unicast links. The participating nodes relay messages sent by other members of the node. A mesh topology is created by each participating node, establishing connections to a subset of the other nodes. Each sender sends out messages to one or more of the neighbors in the overlay, and the messages are relayed by the other participants.

The fundamental design issues are the same as that in network layer multicast, except that an overlay network topology also needs to be generated. The topology may be generated by means of a central server [56] or it may be created using distributed schemes [57, 58]. The participants in the overlay network monitor the characteristics of the links that connect the different sites. The link characteristics are used to determine the links that will make up the overlay, as well as the path along which messages will be routed. When a central server is used, all nodes report the link characteristics they are aware of to the central server. The central server notifies the nodes of the most suitable nodes that each node ought to establish an overlay link with. In a distributed scheme, each node needs to get an initial list of some peer nodes, probe the nodes for link characteristics, and then select a subset of them and establish a point-to-point connection with the selected nodes. The initial list of nodes may be required as an initial condition, or it can be retrieved from a central node with which the participants may register.

Application layer overlays provide a convenient way to obtain multicast in environments in which network layer multicast is not available. They can also be used to bridge two networks with network layer multicast capability that are separated by an intervening network that does not support network layer multicast.

6.4 CDN MANAGEMENT ISSUES

One of the problems associated with content distribution networks is that there are machines spread across a wide area. Each site that is deployed within the CDN, as well as each machine within the CDN, needs to be managed. Management includes taking care of the installation, configuration, and software updates of the various sites in the CDN, as well as consolidating any usage statistics and accounting information available in distributed locations into a single site. Another aspect of CDN management is ensuring that communication between the sites in a CDN is kept secure. In this section, we look at the approaches that can be used to address these concerns.

6.4.1 Configuration Mechanisms for CDN Sites

In order for the CDN sites to operate efficiently, the machines making them up need to be configured appropriately. A single CDN site may consist of several routers, load balancers, firewalls, and servers. Some simple CDN sites may consist only of one single machine. Regardless of the complexity of the site, each machine in the site has to be configured in order to participate in the CDN.

For a relatively large site, one or more administrators can be present locally for the task of administering and managing the different machines at the site. For smaller sites, in particular, sites that have a single machine, the costs of providing a local administrator may be excessive. In these cases, one needs to be able to administer the machines remotely. However, a machine that allows an administrator to log in remotely is more susceptible to a security breach.

Thus, there are two types of CDN sites: those that have local administrators and those that are managed remotely. Let us refer to the first category as manned sites, and the others as unmanned sites.

One option for secure remote management is to have a secure secret path that an administrator can use to access the machines at an unmanned site. As an example, a private secondary network among the CDN sites can provide a secure path for the administrator to access the device. Another option is to have a modem with telephone connectivity at the CDN site. An administrator dials into the modem (which runs at a secret telephone number) in order to gain access to the CDN site administrator functions. The site will then challenge the administrator for a password (or use some other authentication scheme) and allow access on the success of the authentication process. The main limitation of this approach is that it relies on security via obscurity, and the CDN site may be exposed to someone who may happen to stumble onto the telephone line by mistake, e.g., on a misdialed call.

Another option is for a machine in the unmanned CDN site to disallow any inbound calls, but initiate a connection to a manned site. The CDN site software is preconfigured with the location of the site to connect to. Once a CDN site is connected to the manned site, one of the administrators at the manned site performs the requisite configuration of the machine.

The ideal machine at a unmanned CDN site would be self-configuring. It should not require any administration for its initial configuration on-site, and should begin to operate once it is powered on at the CDN site. In case of faulty operation, it should start working correctly after it is power-cycled (i.e., turned off and then on again). A slightly less ideal (but somewhat more realistic) situation would have the device go through a simple preconfiguration stage that performs partial configuration, and then have the device configure itself fully when it is powered on. As an example of a preconfiguration, machines that are to be shipped to a remote site (with no expert administrators on site) are configured at a central site with a standard set of initial software, a unique identity, and parameters needed for basic network connectivity, e.g., an IP address, a DNS address, and the default router. When these devices are installed at the CDN site, they use the preconfigured parameters to obtain network connectivity, and subsequently contact a configuration server to determine the remaining parts of their configuration.

In order for a device to configure itself automatically, it needs to obtain a globally unique identity for itself, discover its role within the entire CDN system, and then configure itself in accordance with that role. For each of these tasks, several different approaches are possible.

The easiest way to obtain a unique identity is to rely on a label that will be hard-wired into the device. The network interface cards on most systems carry a unique identity following the conventions in the networking industry. The simplest way to use the unique identity is to use the address of the network interface card. When a device has many network interface cards, it can choose one of them arbitrarily. As long as the interface card's identity is unique, this step can be performed relatively easily. Otherwise, an identity can be assigned as part of the preconfiguration procedure.

After powering up, the device needs to obtain an IP address and other configuration parameters for it to be able to communicate with the outside world. If the device is in a large site with a DHCP server, then an IP address and other configuration parameters can be obtained from the device from the DHCP server. If the device will be operating in an environment where the DHCP server is not available, the basic configuration required for network connectivity should be part of the preconfiguration.

Once a device has obtained network connectivity, it can obtain its unique identity to contact a configuration server. The location of the configuration server needs to be a part of the preconfiguration. The configuration server contains a mapping from the unique identity of the server to the role that the device is expected to play in the site. This mapping can be created by an administrator at one of the manned sites. The appropriate configuration for machines playing each role can then be retrieved from the configuration server.

6.4.2 Data Management for CDN Sites

One of the critical functions required in many sites is the collection of various types of statistics, e.g., user access frequency and patterns, the performance of the system, and the resource utilization of the different machines in the server. This information is required for billing and accounting purposes, diagnosing performance problems, as well as for longer-term capacity and resource planning. Much of this data needs to be kept in an archive so that it can be analyzed and processed subsequently. Since archiving and backup support is expensive and difficult to provide at all CDN sites, it will need to be done at a central location. One of the manned CDN sites would be a good choice as the location for the archive. Each CDN site will need to send the information to the archive site. A CDN site can use one of two approaches to maintain its statistical data at the archive site: (1) it can maintain the information locally and send it in a batch to the archive site at regular intervals, or (2) it can send the data to the archive site as soon as it is generated. The first option is better from a performance perspective. Backups can be done when the network is not loaded (e.g., in the middle of the night). However, there may be a loss of data if the CDN site fails. The second option (writing data in real time) can slow down users, but is more reliable. The operator of a CDN site will need to determine the right approach for archiving statistics depending on the importance of the statistics.

Any error conditions and exceptional situations that arise in the operation of a CDN also need to be reported back to a manned central site. Error conditions need to be reported in real time rather than in an archival mode. There are three approaches for the collection of error diagnostics in real-time:

1. The first approach is for a program at the central manned site to periodically query the unmanned site for any errors or diagnostic messages that may have been generated since the last polling period.

2. The second approach is for a program at the unmanned site to send the diagnostic information to the central manned site. In this case, the unmanned site must be able to access and invoke a program to send this data to the manned site.

3. The third approach is a combination of the above two. In this case, most of the information is collected by the central manned site using polling. However, in the case of a condition that needs to be handled urgently, the unmanned site sends a notification to the central site requesting that it be polled quickly. The manned site can then poll the unmanned site as quickly as it can.

The advantage of the polling approach is that it produces a balanced load on the central manned site, which can analyze and process diagnostics at its convenience. The drawback of the approach is that each site has to wait for its turn to send the diagnostics. Some error condition at the unmanned site may need immediate attention but will still have to wait until the central manned site connects again. The second approach allows for immediate handling of urgent messages, but has the danger that several unmanned sites can overwhelm the central site by generating too many messages at the same time. The third approach offers an intermediate compromise. The design of most common system management software [59, 60] and the SNMP [61] protocol allows for analogous mechanisms.

6.4.3   Security Issues in CDNs

Three types of security issues need to be considered in the design of a CDN: (1) ensuring the security of each site that is a part of a CDN, (2) ensuring the security of the communication among pairs of CDN sites, and (3) ensuring the security of content that is cached or replicated at the surrogate sites.

Ensuring the security of a CDN site is no different from ensuring the security of any site in a network. A secure CDN site will need to provide for one or more firewalls that will guard against different types of attacks and unauthorized usage. Some of the issues with the use of multiple firewalls in a CDN site were discussed in Chapter 2.

The security of communication between the different CDN sites can be ensured in one of three ways:

1. A secondary private network that is known to be secure be can be established among the different CDN sites, and used for all intersite communication.
2. A virtual private network (VPN) can be established between the CDN sites. This site can be established on the common network using security technologies such as IP-sec [84]. All communication that occurs among the sites on the VPN is encrypted and secured using IP-sec tunnels.
3. All communication among the sites can be encrypted using a secure transport protocol such as SSL [85]. The connections that are established among the CDN sites are authenticated.

All programs communicating between the CDN sites have to use secure transport or otherwise ensure the security of data by encryption at the application layer.

Any type of encryption comes at the cost of degraded performance. On a shared infrastructure that is already congested, encryption makes access between the CDN sites even more expensive. Therefore, CDNs are more likely to be effective in environments in which the content is mostly publicly accessible, or the need to communicate with the other CDN sites is minimized as far as possible.

The third type of security concern in a CDN is related to data that is present at a surrogate site. Some of the data at a surrogate site may be sensitive. Sensitive data may result from a surrogate site caching content that has access control requirements. After all, there is no reason why secure content should not benefit from the presence of caching surrogates. Sensitive data may also result from a surrogate site collecting some information from the users that needs to be handled with caution. With the growing concerns for privacy over the Internet, some of the information, such as user e-mail addresses, needs to be protected from unauthorized access. Given the fact that the security of some of the unmanned sites will not be as strong as that of the manned sites, special attention needs to be given to sensitive content.

There are three approaches to dealing with the sensitive content at the CDN sites. The first one is to ensure that no sensitive data is kept at sites where security may not be very strong. This implies that all user requests that deal with accessing secure pages, or requests that provide sensitive information about the user (e.g., credit card numbers and e-mail addresses) should only be handled by the origin site, which would have enough safeguards in place to handle sensitive data correctly.

The second approach is for all CDN sites to use a central authentication and authorization service. When any access to sensitive content is made, each CDN site checks the central service to authenticate the user and to check if the user should be provided access to the sensitive content. A client accessing a copy of the cached content is only provided the information is he/she is able to present a set of valid credentials. Each site needs to be trusted to handle the user credentials (e.g., passwords) in a safe fashion. If all the CDN sites are administered by the same organization, this approach is quite attractive. The administration of access control lists and user authentication information is localized at the central service. Secure content can be cached at any site, and be provided to a user from a server located close by.

In some CDN deployments, the surrogate sites and the origin site belong to different organizations. As an example, one can consider an enterprise that sells content by subscription utilizing the services of a content distribution service provider that has an extensive network of surrogate servers. Although the enterprise may be willing to trust the service provider with the content, it may not wish to share its lists of subscribers with the service provider, nor is it likely to reveal the set of credentials (passwords) used by subscribers to its system.

In these cases, the third approach to hosting sensitive content can be used. This approach uses the origin site of the CDN for validation of user credentials. Once the origin site has validated the credentials, the origin site issues a ticket to the user. The ticket would contain information about the content the user is allowed to access, and would have a digital cryptographic signature as proof that it came from the origin site. The user can then retrieve the content from a surrogate site within the CDN and present the ticket as a proof of its right to access the content. The surrogate site validates the ticket and provides the content to the user on the presentation of a valid ticket. The model is similar to the Kereberos [86] security architecture, except that it is applied in the context of a content distribution network.

Depending on the environment in which a CDN operates, one of the above three approaches may be used for caching sensitive content at a surrogate site.

7 Applications of Content Distribution Networks

All the preceding chapters have looked at different components of a content distribution network and the different approaches that can be used to build those components. However, they did not address the use of the CDN, and the type of applications that can benefit from running on a CDN. In this chapter, we look at some of the applications that are normally run at a central server but can benefit from the use of a content distribution network.

At the time of the writing of this book, the most prevalent use of CDNs is serving images and multimedia clips from surrogate sites. However, the CDN architecture can be used to benefit many other types of applications. The major benefits of running an application in the CDN environment are improvements in user response time and increase in scalability. Scalability may be measured by the number of users that can be supported concurrently with a reasonable response time.

In the first section of this chapter, we look at the characteristics of applications that can be run advantageously in a CDN environment and the applications that are not suitable for a CDN environment. In the following sections, we look at several applications that are suitable for the CDN environment and discuss how they can be designed to take advantage of the CDN architecture. Given the predominance of the web at the current time, most of the examples deal with web-centric applications.

7.1 APPLICATION SUITABILITY FOR A CDN

The basic goal of a CDN is to improve user responsiveness and to increase the scalability of a system. These objectives are attained by offloading some of the processing functions to a surrogate closer to the end user. The gains in user responsiveness and scalability depend on how good the surrogate is at serving the content.

151

Given a request from the client, the surrogate must be able to service it correctly without needing to access the origin server. If the percentage of requests that are serviced at the surrogate is high, then the surrogate will be able to provide better performance. The surrogate can use a variety of caching schemes (file caching, stream caching, query caching, database table caching, application caching, etc.) to increase the percentage of requests that it can service locally. In order for the surrogate to service the request locally, the type of data being accessed by a request should be cacheable, and the probability of the required data being present in the surrogate cache should be high.

The requirement that data required for a request be resident at the surrogate can be met with high probability under a couple of different assumptions. If the total data present at the origin site is replicated at the surrogate site, the surrogate will always have the data. If only a fraction of the data at the origin site is replicated (or cached) at the surrogate, there would be some cache misses. However, if the access pattern of clients shows preference for a limited fraction of data, then caching can be quite effective. In other words, clients tend to access some data more frequently than others.

Whenever data is maintained with multiple copies, there is a danger of these copies getting out of sync with each other. Therefore, cacheable data must change at a relatively slow rate and some inconsistencies in the data ought to be acceptable. If the data changes slowly, the system can use one of the data coherency approach discussed in Chapter 5 to ensure that the data eventually becomes consistent. The speed/slowness of change ought to be compared against the effectiveness of the cache coherency scheme deployed. Since most data consistency schemes will result in some window of inconsistent data, the limited window of inconsistency should not cause a failure in the application.

If all copies of data need to be always consistent with each other, then one has to use a protocol like the two-phase commit to ensure synchronized updates. Such data is not a good candidate for replicating in a CDN environment since such commit protocols have a very poor performance over a wide area network.

Each application request can either modify the data or simply read it. If the ratio of read requests to write requests is high, then CDN-based approaches can be quite effective. By bringing the data closer to the clients, a CDN can improve the performance of read requests. Some writes—those that only need to operate data at a single surrogate site and do not need synchronization with other sites—will also see improved performance. However, writes that require that data be made consistent with other surrogate sites will activate expensive data consistency protocols and introduce extra overheads. If the fraction of writes is a small fraction of the overall requests, then the overall system will see improved performance.

As an example, consider an online store at which 90% of requests are simply browsing through the store and 10% result in purchases. When done at a central site, each request takes 100 ms to complete from a client's perspective (i.e., from the time the client issues the request to the time the client receives the complete response). If the data is replicated to 10 sites, the clients will see improved response time for reads. The improvement results from the fact that each site is closer to the end user and the load on each server is reduced. Let us say the new time for a read request is 20 ms. If we use the two-phase commit protocol to process writes, each write will see degraded performance, say 200 ms. The new overall time for all requests will be 38 ms, which reduces overall response time by almost a third.

Two points need to be made about the example above. The first is that we assumed that read requests do not need to acquire locks. As a result, two identical requests coming to two different sites at the same time may read different values if an update is in progress. If this is not acceptable, then the reads may need to acquire locks and their response time will also degrade. In that case, a CDN is not the right approach. The second point is that most online stores generate revenues from write requests (e.g., a purchase order) and no revenues from read requests. Therefore, a solution that increases the response time of write requests while improving the response time of read requests is doing something wrong. In this example, the right solution would be to use a CDN for the read requests, but not for the write requests. Let us say that the reads would see a response time of 20 ms, whereas the writes would see one of about 80 ms (because the load on origin server would be much lower). The overall response time is now 26 ms, about a quarter of the initial case.

When applications are executed at surrogate sites in a CDN, an analogous results holds for them. Applications that only access data that is present locally at the surrogate sites, and do not have a strong need for synchronizing with data at other sites, will benefit from the use of CDNs, whereas some other applications may see degraded performance from the use of a CDN. The good news is that many web-based applications can be designed to operate in a manner so as to benefit from a CDN.

In some cases, there may be nontechnical issues that determine whether a request is to be executed at a surrogate site or performed at the origin site. If a request generates data that collects information about a client, it may be subject to privacy laws of different countries. In these cases, it might be better to deal with the data at the origin site in a centralized fashion so that the proper procedures can be enforced. In other cases, licensing agreements may prohibit storing copies of data (such as music files) or applications (e.g., those needing software licenses) at the surrogate sites. Legal and policy issues must be considered when deciding how to split an application between the surrogate sites and the surrogates.

Summarizing, an application may be a good candidate for a CDN if

- It has a high ratio of reads compared to writes
- Client access patterns tend to access some set of objects more frequently
- Limited windows of inconsistent data are acceptable
- Data updates occur relatively slowly

An application is not a good candidate for a CDN if

- It requires strong consistency of data
- It modifies shared data and requires concurrency control
- It has security or licensing needs that require centralization

The above lists provide some rough guidelines for what types of applications can benefit from executing in a CDN environment. Applications can be designed in a way so that some or all of their components benefit from execution in a CDN. In the next few sections, we take a look at some of the applications and how they can benefit from a CDN.

7.2 STATIC WEB PAGES

The first application that we examine is the delivery of web pages over the Internet or a corporate intranet. Any object accessible via a web browser has a URL associated with it. A web page is an object with HTML text and links to other objects. The linked objects fall into two categories. Some of the linked objects are accessed immediately by a web browser when the web page is accessed, whereas other linked objects are accessed only on some explicit action by the user. The former category of linked objects are referred to as embedded objects, and are typically graphics and images that are used to create a visually appealing impression for the user. The embedded objects and links in a page mostly point to objects and web pages on the same server, but they can also point to objects on any other server on the network.

A large component of the user-perceived delay in accessing a page over a network is due to the time it takes to load the embedded objects. In order to improve the performance, these objects can be retrieved from the surrogate sites in a CDN, rather than from the origin site itself. This is done automatically provided the URL for the object references the appropriate surrogate site. The only problem is that the appropriate surrogate site is different for different clients, depending on the location of the client in the network.

There are two common approaches to direct each client to the appropriate server. In the first approach, the URLs for all objects on a CDN use a common name or IP address. As an example, consider an embedded object included in a web page at a site www.originalsite.com with a URL of /images/image1.gif or, equivalently, a URL of www.originalsite.com/images/image1.gif. This URL can be changed to refer to www.surrogatesite.com/images/image1.gif. When a client attempts to access the modified URL, the DNS-based schemes or IP routing based schemes described in Chapter 3 can be used to direct the client to the appropriate CDN site. The surrogate maintains the reverse binding on this mapping and sends the appropriate image on receiving the request.

The second approach is for the origin site to maintain different versions of a page, each version directing the clients to load the embedded graphics from one of the many surrogate sites. The origin site maintains a routing table that determines which version of the page ought to be sent to each of the clients. This approach allows more control over the routing of the clients to the surrogates. The origin site knows the identity of the client making a request and can choose surrogates more precisely than possible with the DNS approach; it does not need close coordination with the network provider as the IP routing approach does. However, it requires more processing at the origin site.

Either of these two approaches can be used with links to other web pages at the origin site, not just for embedded graphics objects. Thus, any web page can be served from the surrogate site, or a web-based program (a cgi-bin program, a JSP, or a Java servlet) can be invoked at the surrogate site. The main problem of offloading pages to a surrogate site arises when a user bookmarks the reference to a surrogate in the browser. The bookmarked reference will always be to the surrogate server, even if the original site decided later not to offload the page or changed the selection of the surrogate for a site (in the second approach). One way to resolve the problem is for the surrogate to introduce a note in the web page with a link to a URL at the origin site asking that users click on that URL before bookmarking the page. Such an approach requires modifications to the web page. Another alternative is for the surrogate sites to redirect such bookmarked references to the origin server if they decide to no longer serve a page from the origin site. This will work provided the named surrogate is not down and the mapping between the URLs seen at the surrogate and the URL at the original web page be maintained forever.

7.3 STREAMING MULTIMEDIA DELIVERY

Multimedia content (audio, video, and animations) on websites can be accessed in one of two ways: either by downloading the entire content to a client and then playing it locally, or by using a streaming server. The streaming server enables a client to start viewing the content much faster, and is the preferred method for long streams or for watching real-time events on a network.

If the surrogate sites implement the function of a multimedia streaming server, such a service can be provided at the surrogate site instead of requiring a client to access the origin site. Network performance can play a critical role in the quality of the stream seen by the client. Anyone who has played multimedia streams over the Internet has encountered a phase in which network congestion has frozen the stream or degraded its quality severely. Since the surrogate sites are much closer to the clients, accessing streams from the cached copy is likely to provide much better performance.

Some multimedia content is associated with restrictions as to who can view it. In these cases, the surrogate sites need to enforce the same access restrictions as the origin site. This requires the surrogate sites to implement support for digital rights management in a manner that is interoperable with the origin site's scheme for digital rights management.

Different types of digital rights architectures are being developed in various industry consortia and by individual corporations. However, at the fundamental level, they consists of three basic functions: (1) a way for the author of the content to specify restrictions on usage, (2) a way to associate usage restrictions with a piece of content and, (3) a way to enforce the access restrictions. Each digital rights management architecture implements these functions in different ways.

When played from a surrogate site, the surrogate sites have to support the latter two functions of digital rights management. They need to obtain the usage restrictions associated with a piece of multimedia content, and to enforce those restrictions. A digital rights management system may bundle the description of the usage restrictions together with the multimedia content, or it may provide mapping from a central location. The enforcement of digital rights is typically done in the player or viewer software for the content at the client. Although some enforcement can also be done by the server, restricting access to authorized clients, it may not prevent a client from making copies of the content.

Let us consider the case in which rights enforcement is part of the player software. The surrogate sites have to provide the player with data containing the content and the digital rights. One way to do this would be to consider the pair of content and associated digital rights as the basic unit of caching. In these cases, the surrogates have to do little more than normal caching of this basic unit.

If the same content is provided to different users with different set of rights, the surrogate site can take on the function of bundling the access rights appropriate to the user with the cached copy of the content. This requires the surrogate to cache only one copy of the content (which is relatively large) and customize it with the right set of access controls depending on who is accessing the content. This requires the origin site to trust the surrogate, and the surrogate has to authenticate the users.

7.4 ADVERTISEMENT GENERATION

Among the components that are often seen on web pages are the banner advertisements that are usually at the header or the footer of a page. These web advertisements are typically generated by a script running at the origin web site or, in many cases, by a third-party advertisement generating company, such as DoubleClick [77] or Fastclick [78]. In order for the generated advertisement to be effective, it must be selected taking into account the preferences of the user accessing the page on which the advertisement is placed.

Systems generating advertisements can be divided into two types. One type generates an advertisement based solely on the contents of the page a user is accessing. The other type maintains a profile for the user, and takes the user profile into account, along with the contents of the page being accessed, to generate the advertisement. The profiles of a user may be obtained in some cases by having the user fill out a registration form. In other cases, the profile of a user can be generated by observing the set of pages the user is likely to follow. In most of these cases, it is possible to move the generation of the advertisements to one of the surrogate sites in a CDN.

Let us consider the first type, in which advertisements are generated based solely on the contents of the page a user is accessing. A user who is accessing the sports page at a newspaper website is presented with advertisements pertaining to sports equipment. In most of these systems, the advertisement generation process can be divided into two steps. In the first step, the different URLs being accessed by a user are mapped into one of many different categories. Each category points to a set of advertisements from which one is selected randomly, or to some other distribution which may display some advertisements more often (probabilistically) than the others.

One useful application of the surrogate site would be to generate advertisements that are intended to target local users. If the CDN routing mechanism maintains some rough degree of geographical proximity, it is likely that most clients accessing a surrogate are from the same geographical region. Thus, a surrogate server can generate advertisements that are targeted for a local audience. A surrogate server located in New York City may generate advertisements for the local basketball team whenever the sports page of a newspaper is accessed, whereas the surrogate server located in San Francisco, California, would generate advertisements for a different team.

In order to generate these advertisements from the surrogate site, the surrogate site needs to know how to map a URL into its category, and then select an advertisement belonging to that category. If we think of the logic mapping the URL to the category as a large table, the surrogate site may cache portions of this table and be able to obtain the right mapping for most URLs from its cache. There are two approaches to caching the URL-to-category mapping table. If the mapping is encoded by a program and the program is relatively simple, it may be possible to execute the same program at the surrogate site. Otherwise, the surrogate site may use a query–result caching scheme in which the output of the program (the category) is cached for each input (URL) that the surrogate site has seen thus far. If there is some locality in how URLs are accessed, this caching scheme can be quite effective. The table or the program defining URL-to-category mapping would be periodically updated as new statistics are collected. However, since such changes are expected to be no more frequent than once a day, caching with simple consistency mechanisms (e.g., expiration time of 1 day) will be good enough to generate a reasonably accurate URL-to-category mapping.

Having determined the category, the surrogate site now needs to select an advertisement. One way to do this would be for the surrogate to maintain a cache of advertisements for each category. One of the advertisements is picked randomly from the cached set of advertisements, and the cached set is refreshed periodically from the origin server. It is relatively simple to design a formula for selecting advertisements according to some weights that will approximate the distribution when all advertisements are serviced from the origin server.

For advertisement generation that takes into account a user profile, the advertisement generation process determines the category of advertisements to be shown based on the URL being accessed, as well as the profile and preferences of the user. If the profile information is available at the surrogate site, the surrogate site can use the same logic to determine the category on the basis of the profile. Another option is to use the query result caching scheme, in which the keys for the query are the URL being accessed, and the identity of the user. As long as the user profile is cached at the surrogate site, the advertisement generation process can be done locally at the edge. Since most CDN routing schemes tend to send a client to the same surrogate site, caching of user profiles is likely to have a very high hit rate.

Even when advertisements are generated by the surrogate sites, a log of all the displayed advertisements needs to be collected at a central site. This log forms the basis on which the different advertisers are billed. Each surrogate site can maintain its own log, and the logs from all the sites can be merged at the central site. The surrogates can send their logs periodically to the central site, or on demand from the central site.

In some cases, the log entry may include a cookie to track the identity of users and to track usage access patterns. A cookie is a piece of data that is set by a server on a user's browser; the browser sends the cookie back to the server on each subsequent request. The server setting the cookie can ask that the cookie be sent to all servers in a DNS domain to which the server belongs. Thus, a server in www.division.company.com can ask that the cookie be sent back only to itself, to any server in domain division.company.com, or any server in domain company.com. It can also ask that the cookie be sent to any server in domain .com but few servers would broadcast it to such a large set. The cookie must be set so that the browser sends it to any surrogate site that the client might be accessing. This requires that all surrogates be in a common DNS domain with the origin site. If a surrogate site is in a different DNS domain, a cookie sharing scheme must be devised to allow tracking a user cookie across multiple DNS domains.

The sharing of cookie information across different domains requires that each domain establish its own cookie at a user. This information can then be correlated with the two domains. As an example, a server in domain 1 can set a cookie assigning a user the identity of idOne. A server in domain 2 may have assigned another cookie to the user with the identity of idTwo. The server in domain 1 can redirect the user to access a resource from the server in domain 2 or load a small image located at a server in domain 2, where the URL identifying the resource or record is of the form server.domain2.com/myid=idOne/image.gif. The user accesses the server in domain 2 with his cookie containing the identity idTwo, and domain 2 can then determine that the user identified as idOne in domain 1 is the same as the user identified as idTwo in domain 2. The servers in each domain may opt to put a common shared identity on the user to track it in a common way across the domain. Any profile information about the user can then be shared among the two domains.

The sharing of a user's profile information can be used by the surrogate servers to generate advertisements as well as customize a page according to the preferences of an individual user.

7.5 CONTENT ADAPTATION

The clients accessing information in the Internet (or an enterprise intranet) include users on a personal computer as well as those using hand-held devices and palmtops. As a result of the variety of access devices, the simple HTML formatted page can no longer fit the needs of all users. Individuals obtaining a web page with their palmtop devices need to access data using the WAP [79] protocol rather than the HTTP protocol that is used by the browsers commonly available on the desktop computers. Even among users accessing the content through normal computers and HTTP, the individual preferences of users may be different. A user in France may want to see a page in French, whereas a user in the United States would prefer to see all pages in English. The content provided by a server must be compatible with the needs of the users.

If a server knows the preferences of a client, it can render the content in the format that is desired and acceptable by the client. However, in many cases, the server may not be able to know the preferences. A server located in the Eastern United States may be accessed by users across the world. It is hard for the server to know the native language of a client unless this information is present in a user profile or a cookie. Not many servers ask for this type of information from a user. On the other hand, if a content distribution network is in place, and multiple surrogate servers are present, a surrogate has a high probability of getting clients with default language preference for the local language. Thus, a surrogate site located in France can translate all documents into French by default, and a surrogate located in Japan can translate all documents into Japanese by default.

Even if the information is available, content adaptation imposes an additional load on the origin site. This load may manifest itself as a need for extra processing power, extra storage, or support of extra functions. In order to support translation, each site needs a translator and must store multiple versions of each document. In order to support WAP users, each site must support the WAP protocol. This additional load can be transferred to the surrogate site, reducing the need for processing cycles at the original location. Having a content distribution network wherein all surrogate sites support the WAP functions implies that the server need not worry about supporting wireless devices. If the same network of surrogate sites is used to support many origin sites, none of the origin sites need to support WAP.

Content adaptation typically operates on a single file or web page at a time. Thus, the functions that perform these changes can be readily provided at the surrogate site. Another option is for the surrogate site to use caching techniques for processed data and cache the modified version of each file/page after the appropriate transformations have been made.

7.6 MAIL SERVER

While dwarfed in actual traffic usage on the Internet and intranets by the users of the web, mail remains one of the key applications enabled by internet technology. A mail server is a machine that stores electronic mail for users, allowing them to read and send mail as needed. A variety of protocols can be used between the user and the mail server. Products such as Microsoft Exchange and Lotus Notes provide their own specialized mail services and use a proprietary protocol between the client and the server. Some of the open protocols that can be used between a client and a mail server include POP (Post Office Potocol) [80] and IMAP (Internet Message Access Protocol) [81]. IMAP allows a user to access a mail database on a remote server. POP is a protocol that allows a user to download a mail database from a remote server to the local file system. Some mail servers allow access to the user's mail through web browsers over HTTP. When mail servers need to exchange mail belonging to different users, they typically use the SMTP (Simple Mail Transfer Protocol) [18].

Most Internet service providers as well as many other sites on the Internet provide mail service to their users. Let us consider the structure of one of these sites. The mail provider site would be located somewhere on the Internet, enabling access to all of its users. Some of the well-known public mail servers on the Internet include Hotmail (www.hotmail.com) and Yahoo (www.yahoo.com). They provide a service by which any user of the Internet can access their mail using a standard web browser. One way to implement this service is to have a web server with programs that access the back-end mail server using the IMAP protocol.

When a user is in a remote location, the perceived performance of the mail server can become rather poor. In that case, the performance can be improved significantly by moving the web server closer to the client by exploiting a CDN. In these cases, the web server provides better mail access to the clients by caching their content closer to them.

In order for the scheme to work well, clients should typically be accessing the same surrogate site for extended periods. When a client is first directed to a surrogate site, the surrogate site obtains the mail file belonging to the client and caches it locally. It may use a protocol like POP to implement this function. The client manipulates the mail file on the surrogate server, using the surrogate to read, send, or delete mail messages. At periodic intervals, the mail databases maintained at the surrogate sites are synchronized back to the mail servers at the origin site.

Two features need special considerations with respect to the access of mail at the surrogate sites. The first is the issue of registration, and the second is that of authenticating a client. When a new user arrives in the system, should registration be handled by the original site or by the surrogate site? Both of these solutions are technically viable, except that the profile information of the mail user would be visible to the CDN site in the second case. If the CDN site belongs to a different administrative domain (e.g., the CDN is provided by a third party), the approach of restricting registration to the central site would be the preferred approach. In the same environment, the origin site may not want the surrogate to see the passwords used by the clients. In that case, the schemes described for secure content caching in Chapter 6 need to be used to hide the credentials of the mail users from the surrogate sites. Using this approach, the client would first need to authenticate itself with the origin site. The origin site would issue the client a ticket that can be used to access its mail database at the surrogate site. The tickets can be carried in this specific example as cookies in the HTTP protocol.

The mail server application above assumes that only one user is accessing the mail database at any time. If two people share a single mail database, they may see inconsistent views of the database as each person manipulates the database independently. The synchronization can be done relatively easily using locking and is a nonissue if the two happen to access the same database at the same surrogate site. However, if they are directed to different surrogate sites, the synchronization needed would degrade performance tremendously. Thus, the performance gains require that each database be cached only at a single surrogate site. If the initial log-in of each user is checked with the origin site, and the origin site maintains a table mapping each database to the surrogate that is caching it, this criterion can easily be maintained. When two users try to access the same mail database, they can be directed to the same surrogate site, or the origin site may decide to handle such requests itself. In the latter case, it needs to notify the surrogate that is currently caching the database to not cache it any longer. If there are no active uses of the database at the cache, the surrogate can simply remove the cache. If there are any active users of the database, the surrogate will need to act as a surrogate for the origin site for the current sessions of these users.

7.7 SHOPPING SITES

One of the most common types of sites on the Internet are the online stores that offer electronic sales of items ranging from books, CDs, and software to airline tickets and even everyday grocery items. The performance of many of these sites can be improved significantly by the use of a CDN.

There are some observations that one can make about most online stores. In most online stores, most of the users typically browse through the catalogues rather than make actual purchases. Somewhere between 80% to 90% of the total accesses of an online store are reads and search requests through a catalogue. Only a small percentage of users actually purchase items from the store. However, the browsing users can interfere with the performance of the purchasers, and everyone can get a poor performance when many users are concurrently active at the online store.

The purchasers at the store need to provide information such as their credit card numbers, mailing address, etc., which needs to be handled in a secure fashion. Any information collected by the site regarding mailing addresses and telephone numbers also needs to be handled in accordance with the privacy policies and guidelines established by the site. As a result, it is best to keep the purchasing activities confined to the central origin site. At a single site, it is easier to maintain security and privacy policies, and to implement processes (e.g., audits) that ensure compliance with the policies.

The browsing function is a read-only operation and can be moved to the surrogate sites within a CDN. A user can browse through the entire catalogue or search for a specific page. The surrogate site can satisfy these requests by either maintaining a replicated copy of the entire catalogue or by using query caching techniques. Query caching will work well provided there are some types of queries that are performed more frequently than others.

In a real on-line store, a necessary function associated with browsing is the maintenance of a shopping cart. A client adds items to the online shopping cart while browsing through the catalogue. Moving the browsing function to the surrogate sites would not be effective without moving the shopping cart functions as well. Fortunately, the manipulation of the shopping cart requires updates or changes to information that is unique to each user and does not require any synchronization. Thus, a surrogate can maintain the shopping cart operation for the browsing clients. When the customer is ready to purchase the items in the shopping cart, she or he would be sent to the back-end site.

The only remaining issue is the transmission of the shopping cart contents to the origin site without requiring the customer to provide a credit card number or account information to the surrogate site. There are a variety of ways to solve this problem. The simplest solution would be for the surrogate site to generate a unique identity for the shopping cart, and include this identity and the address of the surrogate site in the URL to the origin site that the client will be accessing to make the checkout. The origin site can then obtain the contents of the shopping cart from the surrogate site using this identity, or the surrogate site may report the contents of the shopping cart to the origin site using this identity when the user begins the checkout process, and subsequently redirect the user with its unique identity to the origin site to complete the checkout.

7.8 CONCLUSIONS

In this chapter, we have looked at some of the ways in which different web-based applications can be designed in order to take advantage of a content distribution network. The examples are meant to be illustrative, not exhaustive. Many other web-based applications, such as on-line auctions, search engines, real estate brokerage sites, etc. can also be designed to exploit CDNs. The concept can also be used for nonweb applications. Applications that exploit CDNs can be built over protocols other than HTTP.

In general, any application that has a large percentage of read-only operations and can operate without strong consistency in its data can gain in performance by exploiting the CDN architecture.

8   Related Topics

This book has primarily examined mechanisms that can be used to create and operate content distribution networks. Many interesting and important areas related to content distribution networks are not covered fully in this book. This chapter provides a brief overview of some related information that should be of interest to you.

Topics that we will examine briefly include the issue of content distribution standards and ad hoc content distribution networks.

8.1   CONTENT DISTRIBUTION STANDARDS

At the time of the writing of this book, no dominant standard on content distribution had emerged, although work on standards related to content distribution was progressing in several industrial consortiums and forums, primarily the IETF (Internet Engineering Task Force). Standards in the IETF are defined by working groups, which consists of people interested in a specific topic. Before a working group is formed, a topic is discussed in a BOF (Birds of a Feather) session. At the time of the publication of this book, there were one working group and two BOFs dealing with issues related to CDNs. Both of the BOFs are expected to become working groups subsequently.

The WEBI (Web Intermediaries) working group [62] is trying to define a protocol that can be used for keeping web resources updated consistently in web-based proxy servers. The same group is also attempting to define the requirements for a protocol that would be needed to discover intermediary surrogate servers. The OPES BOF was exploring opportunities to develop a working group on OPES (open extensible proxy services). The OPES working group will define the architecture of an extensible surrogate that would be able to perform different types of functions at a surrogate site within a CDN. The CDI (Content Distribution Internetworking) BOF was looking at issues related to peering among content distribution networks and defining mechanisms for distribution and routing of requests to the surrogates.

There are two industry consortia trying to define protocols related to content distribution. One is the ICAP Forum [63] led by Akamai, the other is the Content Alliance [64] led by Cisco. The participants in the ICAP forum are active in the IETF OPES BOF, and the Content Alliance partners make significant contributions to the CDI BOF. It is hoped that the IETF working groups will eventually define an interoperable standard for the working of content distribution networks.

As must be apparent from the above, most of the standards activities are in a very early stage and it will be a while before something concrete emerges.

8.2 PEER-TO-PEER CONTENT DISTRIBUTION NETWORKS

The term content distribution network is sometimes applied to ad hoc peer-to-peer networks that can be formed by several independent machines communicating to form an overlay network. Peer-to-peer networks have gained a lot of popularity due to their use in the exchange of digital music files over the Internet, and there are several projects devoted to them [65–68].

A peer-to-peer network consists of many computers that are interconnected in an ad hoc manner. Instead of the traditional client–server model, in which a client retrieves a file from a well-known server, the file may be obtained from any of the machines participating in the peer-to-peer network. In order to obtain content in the peer-to-peer network, a user starts out with a description of the attributes of the information that he/she may be searching for. The next step is to locate a machine in the network that has the file matching the desired attributes. Then the file is retrieved.

In order to locate the appropriate content, one of two approaches can be used. The first approach is to use a central directory server. Each participant reports the type of files it has to a directory server, and anyone looking for information can search the directory server for the matching files and their location. This was the approach used by Napster [66] for their file-sharing program. The other approach is to form an overlay network connecting all the participants. A query from a participant is broadcast along the network until a file matching the query is found. Then the file is sent to the originator of the query.

The formation of the overlay network in the second approach can be done in a number of different ways. Using some offline means, a participant can learn the identity of one or more existing participants in the overlay and join some of the existing participants. Another option is to use a central registration server with which some of the participants have registered and are able to determine who else is participating in the network. One other option is for all participants to use a distributed algorithm to create a spanning tree among themselves.

The broadcasting of the message can also be done in a number of ways. The simplest option is to use flooding. This is the approach used in the Gnutella software [68]. Each participant forwards the query to all other participant it is connected to. Flooding schemes require a way to avoid packets looping forever, e.g., limiting the total number of hops a query will be propagated to, or having each node only process queries it has seen for the first time. The former can be done using a time-to-live field along with the query, which is incremented at every node; the query is discarded if the field increases beyond a fixed threshold. IP forwarding uses a similar technique, except that packets start with a fixed value of the time-to-live field, the value is decremented at every hop, and the packet is discarded if the field reaches zero.

If each node needs to process a query only once, a node needs to remember the query it has seen or a query needs to contain the nodes it has already traversed. Both of these schemes will require space, either in the query or at a node. This requires placing a limit on the size of the space requirement. Since limiting the space opens a window for large loops to exist, these must be used with the time-to-live approach. As an example, if a query has a time-to-live limit of K hops, the number of nodes it needs to remember need not be more than K. If a query contains a list of nodes it has traversed, some duplicate processing can still occur if the query reaches the same node through two different paths.

Flooding is an extreme form of routing that requires very little coordination among participants. Less extreme forms of routing can be used for forwarding requests, and examples of such routing mechanisms can be found in the different approaches to application layer multicasting discussed in Chapter 6.

References

1. D. Menasce and V. Almeida, *Scaling for E-Business: Technologies, Models, Performance, and Capacity Planning,* Upper Saddle River, NJ: Prentice Hall, 2000.

2. H. Jackson and N. Frigon, *Fulfilling Customer Needs: A Practical Guide to Capacity Management,* New York: Wiley, 1998.

3. S. Lam and K. Chan, *Computer Capacity Planning: Theory & Practice,* Orlando, FL: Academic Press, 1987.

4. T. Browning, *Capacity Planning for Computer Systems,* New York: Bantam Books, 1993.

5. M. Schwartz, *Computer Communication Network Design and Analysis,* Englewood Cliffs, NJ: Prentice Hall, 1977.

6. R. Cahn, *Wide Area Network Design,* San Francisco: Morgan Kaufmann Publishers, 1998.

7. A. Kershenbaum, *Telecommunication Network Design Algorithms,* New York: McGraw-Hill, 1993.

8. R. Ellis, *Designing Data Networks,* Englewood Cliffs, NJ: Prentice Hall, 1986.

9. P. Rhodes, *Building a Network: How to Specify, Design, Procure and Install a Corporate LAN,* New York: McGraw-Hill, 1996.

10. H. Dutton and P. Lenhard, *Asynchronous Transfer Mode (ATM): Technical Overview,* Upper Saddle River, NJ: Prentice Hall, ISBN 0135204461, 1995.

11. R. Braden et al., *Resource ReSerVation Protocol (RSVP) Version 1—Functional Specification,* Internet Engineering Task Force RFC 2205, September 1997.

12. D. Matusow, *SNA, APPN, HPR, and TCP/IP Integration,* New York: McGraw-Hill, 1996.

13. S. Blake et al. *An Architecture for Differentiated Services,* Internet Engineering Task Force RFC 2475, December 1998.

14. P. Ferguson and G. Huston, *Quality of Service: Delivering QoS on the Internet and in Corporate Networks,* New York: Wiley, 1998.

15. K. Kilkki, *Differentiated Services,* New York: Macmillan Technical Publishing, 1999.

16. J. Miller, *World Wide Web Consortium PICS Specifications,* Iuniverse.com, ISBN 0595137644, December 2000.

17. G. Marin et al., Overview of the NBBS Architecture, *IBM Systems Journal, 34,* 4, 1995.

18. J. Klensin, *Simple Mail Transfer Protocol,* Internet Engineering Task Force RFC 2821, April 2001.

19. R. Fielding et al., *"Hypertext transport protocol—HTTP/1.1,"* Internet Engineering Task Force RFC 2068, January 1997.

20. T. Agarwala, et al., SP2 System Architecture, *IBM Systems Journal, 34,* 2, 1995.

21. D. Comer, *Internetworking with TCP/IP Vol. I: Principles, Protocols, and Architecture,* Upper Saddle River, NJ: Prentice Hall, 1995.

22. *Overview of the Tiny Web Server,* available at URL http://wearables.stanford.edu/.

23. D. Maltz and P. Bhagwat, *TCP/IP Splicing for Application Layer Proxy Performance,* IBM T. J Watson Research Report number RC21139, March 17th, 1998.

24. M. Leech et al., *SOCKS Protocol Version 5,* Internet Engineering Task Force RFC1928, March 1996.

25. J. Postel, *Internet Control Message Protocol,* Internet Engineering Task Force RFC0792, September 1981.

26. C. Huitema, *Routing in the Internet,* Upper Saddle River, NJ: Prentice Hall, 1995.

27. B. Krishnamurthy and J. Wang, On Network-Aware Clustering of Web Clients, *Proceedings of ACM SIGCOMM 2000,* August 2000.

28. B. Callaghan, *NFS Illustrated,* Reading, MA: Addison Wesley, 1999.

29. J. Bloomer, *Power Programming with RPC,* Cambridge, MA: O'Reilly, 1992.

30. E. Pitt and K. Mcniff, *Java.RMI—The Remote Method Invocation API,* Reading, MA: Addisson Wesley, 2001.

31. G. Reese, *Database Programming with JDBC,* Cambridge, MA: O'Reilly, 2000.

32. J. Siegel, *CORBA 3 Fundamentals and Programming,* New York: Wiley, 2000.

33. M. Baentsch, G. Molter, and P. Sturm, Introducing Application-level Replication and Naming into today's Web, *Computer Networks and ISDN Systems, 28,* 6, 19XX.

34. M. Wiesmann, et al., Database Replication Techniques: A Three Parameter Classification, *Proceedings of 19th IEEE Symposium on Reliable Distributed Systems* (SRDS2000), Nurenberg, Germany, October 2000.

35. M. Wiesmann et al., Understanding Replication in Databases and Distributed Systems, *Proceedings of the 20th International Conference on Distributed Computing Systems,* ICDCS, 2000.

36. D. Wessels, *Web Caching,* Cambridge, MA: O'Reilly, 2001.

37. B. Krishnamurthy and J. Rexford, *Web Protocols and Practice/ HTTP 1.1— Networking Protocols, Caching, and Traffic Measurement,* Reading, MA: Addison Wesley, 2001.

38. R. Strom et al., Gryphon: An Information Flow Based Approach to Message Brokering. *International Symposium on Software Reliability Engineering,* 1998.

39. J. Challenger, et al., A Publishing System for Efficiently Creating Dynamic Web Content, *Proceedings of IEEE INFOCOM 2000,* Tel Aviv, Israel, March 2000.

40. R. Elmasri and S Navathe, *Fundamentals of Database Systems,* Reading, MA: Addision Wesley, 1999.

41. *Real Servers Administration Guide,* Available at URL http://service.real.com/ help/library/guides/server8/realsrvr.htm.

42. D. Le Gall, MPEG: A Video Compression Standard for Multimedia Applications, *Communications of the ACM, 34,* 4, 47–58, 1991.

43. R. Rejaie et al., Multimedia Proxy Caching Mechanism for Quality Adaptive Streaming Applications in the Internet, *Proceedings of IEEE Infocom 2000,* Tel-Aviv, Israel, March 2000.

44. P. Deshpande, et al., Caching Multidimensional Queries Using Chunks, *Proceedings of ACM SIGMOD,* 1998.

45. T. Howes and M. Smith, *LDAP: Programming Directory-Enabled Applications with Lightweight Directory Access Protocol,* New York: Macmillan Technical Publishing, 1997.

46. *UUNET Service Level Agreement,* URL http://www.uunet.net/customer/sla/.

47. H. Ohsaki, et al., Analysis of Rate-Based Congestion Control for ATM Networks, *Proceedings of ACM SIGCOMM,* April 1995.

48. R. Panabaker, S. Wegerif, and D. Zigmond, *The Transmission of IP Over the Vertical Blanking Interval of a Television Signal,* Internet Engineering Task Force RFC 2728, November 1999.

49. M. Luby et al., Practical Loss-Resilient Codes, *Proceedings of ACM Symposium on Theory of Computing,* 1997.

50. J Beyers et al., A Digital Fountain Approach to Reliable Distribution of Bulk Data, *Proceedings of ACM SIGCOM,* Vancouver, Canada, September 1998.

51. L. Rizzo, Effective Erasure Codes for Reliable Computer Communication Protocols, *ACM Computer Communication Review, 27,* 24–36, April 1997.

52. D. Waitzman, C. Partridge, and S. Deering, *Distance Vector Multicast Routing Protocol (DVMRP),* Internet Engineering Task Force RFC 1075, November 1988.

53. J. Moy, *Multicast Extensions to OSPF,* Internet Engineering Task Force RFC 1584, March 1994.

54. D. Estrin et al., *Protocol Independent Multicast-Sparse Mode,* Internet Engineering Task Force RFC 2362, June 1998.

55. Internet Engineering Task Force Working Group on Reliable Multicast Transport Protocol. Charter available at http://www.ietf.org/html.charters/ rmt-charter.html.

56. D. Pendarakis et al., ALMI: An Application Level Multicast Infrastructure, *Proceedings of the Third USENIX Symposium on Internet Technologies and Systems (USITS),* 2001.

57. P. Francis, *Your Own Internet Distribution,* Project description at URL http://www.aciri.org/yoid/.

58. Y. Chu, S. Rao, and H. Zhang, A Case for End System Multicast, *Proceedings of SIGMETRICS 2000,* 2000.

59. R. Lendernmann et al., *An Introduction to Tivoli's TME 10,* Upper Saddle River, NJ: Prentice Hall, 1997.

60. R. Sturm, *Working with Unicenter TNG,* Que Education and Training, 1998.

61. W. Stallings, *SNMP, SNMPV2 and RMON, Practical Network Management,* Reading, MA: Addison-Wesley, 1996.

62. Internet Engineering Task Force Working Group on Web Intermediaries. Charter available at http://www.ietf.org/html.charters/webi-charter.html.

63. Internet Content Adaptation Protocol Forum, URL http://i-cap.org.

64. Content Alliance Forum, http://www.content-peering.org/.

65. F. Dabek et al., Building Peer-to-Peer Systems with Chord, *Proceedings of Eighth IEEE Workshop on Hot Topics in Operating Systems* (HotOS-VIII), May 2001.

66. *Napster protocol specification,* URL http://opennap.sourceforge.net/napster. txt, June 2000.

67. I. Clarke et al., Freenet: A distributed anonymous information storage and retrieval system. *Proceedings of the ICSI Workshop on Design Issues in Anonymity and Unobservability,* Berkeley, California, June 2000. http:// freenet.sourceforge.net.

68. *Gnutella.* http://gnutella.wego.com/.

69. P. Mishra and H. Kanakia, A Hop by Hop Rate-based Congestion Control Scheme, *Proceedings of SIGCOMM '92,* August 1992, pp. 112–123.

70. J. Knight and S. Guest, Using Multicast Communications to Distribute Code and Data in Wide Area Networks, *Software Practice and Experience, 25,* 5, 1995.

71. IBM Corporation, *Page Detailer,* distributed with IBM WebSphere Studio, URL http://www.ibm.com/software/webservers, June 2000.

72. Keynote Systems, Company description at http://www.keynote.com.

73. Gomez Networks, Company description at http://www.gomeznetworks. com.

74. W. Fenner, *Internet Group Management Protocol—Version 2.* Internet Engineering Task Force RFC 2236, November 1997.

75. A. Shaikh, R. Tewari, and M. Agrawal, On the Effectiveness of DNS-based Server Selection, *Proceedings of IEEE INFOCOM, 2001,* April 2001.

76. V. Padmanabhan and L. Subramanian, Determining the Geographic Location of Internet Hosts, *Proceedings of ACM SIGCOM 2001,* 2001.

77. DoubleClick Inc., Company information at http://www.doubleclick.net.

78. Fastclick Inc, Company Information at http://www.fastclick.com.

79. M. van der Heijden and M. Taylor, *Understanding WAP: Wireless Applications, Devices, and Services,* Norwood, MA: Artech House, 2000.

80. J. Myers and M. Rose, *Post Office Protocol—Version 3,* Internet Engineering Task Force RFC 1939, May 1996.

81. M. Crispin, *Internet Message Access Protocol—Version 4rev1,* Internet Engineering Task Force RFC 2060 , December 1996.

82. R. Droms and T. Lemon, *The DHCP Handbook,* Pearson Higher Education, 1999.

83. C. Perkins, *IP Mobility Support,* Internet Engineering Task force RFC 2002, October 1996.

84. S. Kent and R. Atkinson, *Security Architecture for the Internet Protocol,* Internet Engineering Task Force RFC 2408, November 1998.

85. T. Dierks and C. Allen, *The TLS Protocol Version 1.0,* Internet Engineering Task Force RFC 2246, January 1999.

86. B. Tung, *Kereberos: A Network Authentication System,* Addison Wesley, 1999.

Index